DISNEP PRESENTS A PIXAR FILM

THE INCREDIBLES

PRIMA OFFICIAL GAME GUIDE

Ron Dulin

Prima Games
A Division of Random House, Inc.

3000 Lava Ridge Court
Roseville, CA 95661
1-800-733-3000
www.primagames.com

Product Manager: Mario De Govia
Project Editor: Kate Abbott

ISBN: 0-7615-4774-6
Library of Congress Catalog Card Number: 2004109796
Printed in the United States of America
04 05 06 07 LL 10 9 8 7 6 5 4 3 2 1

Acknowledgments: The author would like to thank Kathy Mendoza, Trent Hershenson, and Kirk Somdal from THQ, and AJ Hernandez and Jeff Berting from Heavy Iron, for their help in preparing this book. Extra special thanks to Heavy Iron's Steve Townsend and Kristian Davila for providing invaluable assistance throughout the process.

CONTENTS

MEET THE INCREDIBLES

Play as the Incredibles family in Disney presents a Pixar film, *The Incredibles* video game. You can attack your enemies with super strength as Mr. Incredible; kick, punch, and roll to stop the bad guys with Mrs. Incredible's elasticity; use your invisibility and force field to defend yourself as Violet; and outrun danger with your super speed as Dash. Experience all of their unique powers as you make your way through over 20 levels of gameplay.

In this section we will introduce you to each family member and their skills giving you inside tips on how to best use them.

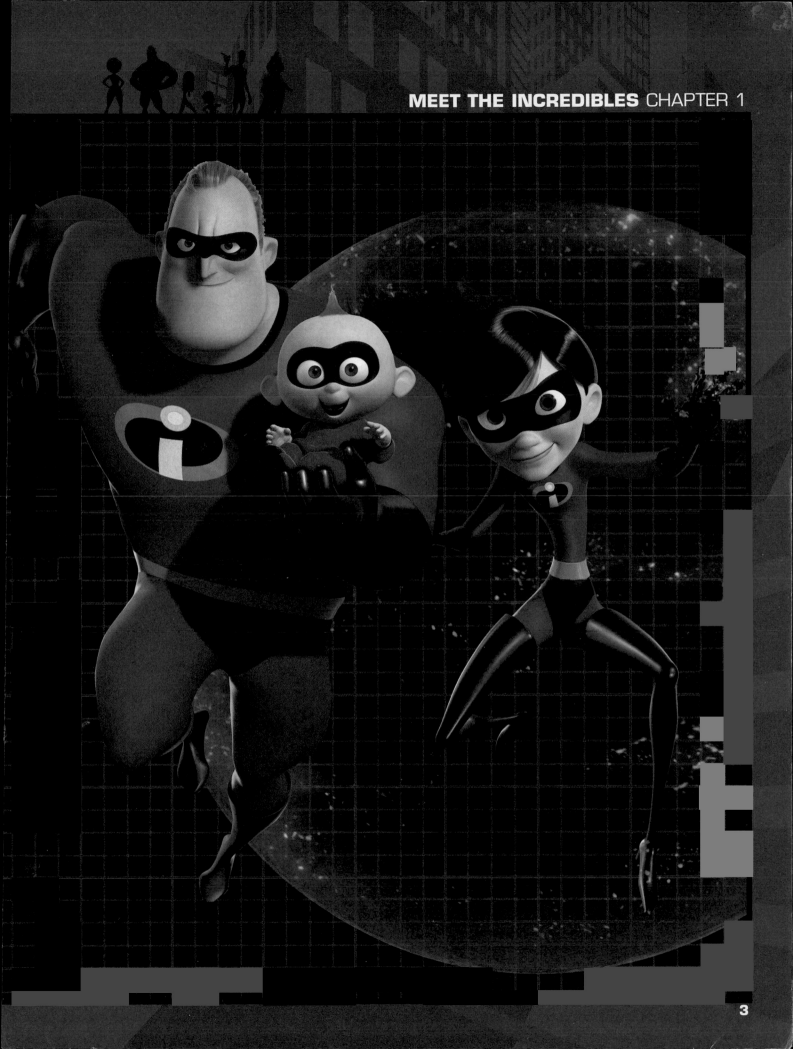

BASIC COMBAT

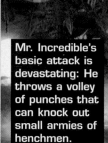

Mr. Incredible's basic attack is devastating: He throws a volley of punches that can knock out small armies of henchmen.

TIP

Use the basic attack several times in succession to create a combination of punches.

INCREDI-PUNCH

Even stronger than his standard attack is his powerful Incredi-Punch. The Incredi-Punch does more damage if Mr. Incredible has Incredi-Power. He gains Incredi-Power by attacking with his standard punch or by picking up Incredi-Power icons.

If Mr. Incredible uses an Incredi-Punch while jumping, he delivers a powerful blow to the ground, which knocks down every enemy in the vicinity.

MR. INCREDIBLE

NAME: BOB PARR
POWER: SUPERHUMAN STRENGTH

Mr. Incredible has a surplus of brawn. His powers and abilities all revolve around his unbelievable strength, which also makes him the best combat-ant in the family. His strength is used for more than just fighting, though; he can also jump immense distances when the need arises.

NOTE

The Incredibles icon in the top left corner of the screen shows important information about your currently active hero. The outer portion of the icon shows the character's health, and the blue lines in the center show his or her current Incredi-Power. The "i" in the center has a different meaning for each character.

TIP

You can "charge" Mr. Incredible's Incredi-Punches by holding down the button. When you release, the blow is even more devastating. Charging an Incredi-Punch consumes more Incredi-Power.

TAP ⊙ REPEATEDLY TO LIFT

THROWING

Mr. Incredible can lift some objects and throw them. This is very helpful when dealing with airborne opponents and for attacking opponents at long range.

Mr. Incredible can throw things farther than normal if necessary. To do so, pick up an object, and then press the Incredi-Punch button instead of the standard throw button.

CONTEXT-SPECIFIC ACTIONS

Throughout his adventures, Mr. Incredible occasionally comes upon markers. Stand on these to perform special actions.

One of these actions is his Incredi-Jump. In some situations, Mr. Incredible can leap off poles and other objects, clearing enormous distances.

Mr. Incredible can also make himself into a human catapult. When prompted, he can grab trees or poles and fling himself high into the air.

He's often called upon to manipulate devices, such as the cranes pictured here. When needed, he can grab onto the device and use his immense strength to rotate it.

Mr. Incredible can also lift extremely heavy objects. Stand on the marker near the object to begin lifting. Watch the Incredibles icon in the top left corner—the "i" in the center tells you how close he is to finishing the job.

TIP

Want to take out more than one enemy? Pick up enemies and throw them at their cohorts! Bulls-eye!

THE INCREDIBLES

MRS. INCREDIBLE

NAME: HELEN PARR
POWER: ELASTICITY

Mrs. Incredible can use her amazing flexibility for strategic and combat purposes. With a variety of fighting moves, Mrs. Incredible is all about versatility. She may not have her husband's strength, but she is quite a formidable opponent.

Before officially becoming Mrs. Incredible, Helen was one of the toughest superheroes around. Watch out for her super stretch punch—it will catch you off guard!

BASIC COMBAT

Mrs. Incredible uses a wide range of close-range fighting moves: kicks, punches, and even rolls. As with Mr. Incredible, using her standard attacks helps build up her Incredi-Power.

INCREDI-PUNCH

Her Incredi-Punch is a sight to behold. When used, she spins around rapidly, stretching her arms out and hitting everything within range.

THROWING

While it can be used to pick up small objects and throw them, her throwing ability is best used in combat. Grab an opponent and swing him around, then let him fly. You can even send him hurtling into other opponents!

STRETCH PUNCH

One of Mrs. Incredible's most useful, and most powerful, attacks is her stretch punch. When it's executed, she extends her arm a great distance and delivers a powerful blow.

GRAPPLING

The levels in which you play Mrs. Incredible are typically more puzzle-oriented than those in which you play Mr. Incredible. You must often employ her ability to grab onto objects. Mrs. Incredible often needs to grab lamps or poles to swing across gaps, and sometimes she needs to grapple moving objects to be carried to a new location.

VIOLET

NAME: VIOLET PARR
POWERS: INVISIBILITY AND
FORCE FIELD

Violet is the daughter of Mr. and Mrs. Incredible. She is the only member of the family with two known powers and a great way to avoid fighting: She can turn herself invisible and also defend herself with a force field! Watch out when she and Dash team up inside the force field to form the Incredi-Ball. Together they are unstoppable!

INVISIBILITY

Violet's ability to turn invisible helps her avoid getting attacked. You need to sneak by a number of enemies and escape a heavily guarded compound. Her invisibility only lasts for a short time, and quickly consumes her Incredi-Power. In "Violet's Crossing" you need to sneak by a number of enemies and escape a heavily guarded compound without running out of energy.

TIP

Violet's Incredi-Power automatically replenishes. Find places to hide and allow it to recharge when playing as her.

DASH

NAME: DASHIELL PARR
POWER: AMAZING SPEED

Dash lives up to his name: This speedy kid can run at 90 miles an hour at a normal sprint and even faster than that when using his Incredi-Boost!

JUMPING

The two Dash levels are basically high-speed obstacle courses. Use his ability to jump to clear small obstructions in his path.

INCREDI-BOOST

Dash's Incredi-Boost temporarily increases his velocity. You can't use your Incredi-Boost for long. Watch the Incredibles icon in the top left corner to make sure Dash still has power. Grabbing the Incredi-Power icon allows Dash more time to run.

TIP

To clear longer distances, use Dash's Incredi-Boost before a jump.

INCREDI-BALL

When Violet and Dash team up, they form the Incredi-Ball. This powerful sphere can do a great deal of damage to objects it smashes into.

The Incredi-Ball doesn't have any active attacks, but if you roll into enemies it does a great deal of damage and sends them flying through the air.

HELPFUL ITEMS

HEALTH

Health power-ups, shaped like a cross in an oval, replenish some of a character's health. When you're hurt, this is what you want. There are three types of health power-ups. Red replenishes your health 50 percent, yellow replenishes it 25 percent, and green replenishes it 10 percent.

INCREDI-POWER ICONS

These icons are shaped like the Incredibles logo. Pick them up and they add a bit of Incredi-Power to a character. There are two varieties. The orange and yellow two-tone Incredi-Power icons add 50 percent to a character's Incredi-Power meter, and the all-yellow ones add 10 percent.

BONUS ITEMS

Each level has three bonus items. These unlock art-work in the gallery (eight per character in Battle Mode), which you can access from the main menu. You have to do some hunting to find most of them!

ENEMIES

In this section, we look at the enemies that try to stop The Incredibles as they attempt to save the world. The game features a wide variety of foes, from human minions to towering, powerful robots. Learn what you're up against before you're up against it by reading the following descriptions and tips!

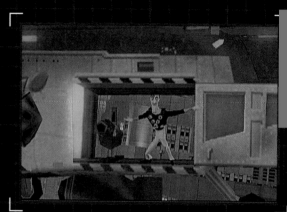

HENCHMEN

Henchmen run the gamut from glass-jawed guards to formidable, armored opponents. They do the bad guys' dirty work for them, and you face enough of them to staff an army. Let's look at the different types of henchmen individually.

HENCHMEN

These guys aren't tough, but they're plentiful. Hone your combat skills against these basic henchmen, the minions of Bomb Voyage, in the beginning of the game. Defeat them with standard attacks and Incredi-Punches.

LOBBER HENCHMEN

Standard henchmen with better equipment, lobber henchmen lob grenades at the heroes from great distances. Watch out they can surprise you in the dense Nomanisan jungle. Pick up their grenades quickly and throw them back. Otherwise, use ranged attacks, like Mr. Incredible's throwing ability, or Mrs. Incredible's stretch punch.

BOMB-TOSSING HENCHMEN

While chasing Bomb Voyage watch out for these crafty henchmen minions who can toss bombs from great distances. The best way to combat them is by picking up their bombs and throwing them back. As Mr. Incredible you can pick up building debris or boxes to throw at them; as Mrs. Incredible use your stretch punch. Remember to be quick!

ARSONISTS

These pyromaniacs only appear in the "Apartment Inferno" level. They are armed with flamethrowers and are fairly difficult to attack head on. When they stop firing for a brief moment, you can rush in and fight. But it's best to either throw objects at them or jump over them and attack from behind.

BOMB VOYAGE FLYING HENCHMEN

That Bomb Voyage has a versatile crew on board. The flying henchman are armed with guns as they hold onto a thin parasol propeller. Use Mrs. Incredible's stretch punch or her grab-and-throw techniques. Mr. Incredible must rely throwing building debris or bombs from the bomb-tossing henchmen. If they fly low enough he can jump up and punch them.

NOMANISAN FLYING HENCHMEN

Armed with missile launchers you don't want to run into these flying baddies. Use Mr. Incredibles throwing abilites and Mrs. Incredible's stretch punch to stop them. Make sure you don't get too close.

NOMANISAN ISLAND HENCHMEN

The standard grunt on Nomanisan Island is tougher than those henchmen you encounter early in the game. However they're easily defeated, so use standard attacks on them unless you're overwhelmed, in which case use Incredi-Punches or ranged attacks.

TIP

When facing missile launcher-equipped flying henchman, jump over their missiles as they get close.

LASER GUN HENCHMEN

A subset of standard henchmen, laser gun henchmen are (surprise!) henchmen armed with laser guns. Laser guns can do a good deal of damage, especially if you wait until you're close to attack. Up close, they use their guns as melee weapons. When possible, used ranged attacks to take them out.

ARMORED HENCHMEN

These guys are the toughest henchmen. They take a great deal of damage before staying down. Mr. Incredible is the only character to face them in the regular game levels. If there are only a few of them, they can be attacked with standard punches, though it takes quite a few to put one down. For larger groups, it's best to rely on Incredi-Punches, and charged ones at that.

THE INCREDIBLES

VELOCIPODS
These henchmen-driven flying vehicles fire missiles and are generally a big nuisance. A human-operated cousin to the automated velocibots, velocipods cause trouble for Dash in "100-Mile Dash," and make an appearance in the "Incredi-Ball" level as well.

BLADEBOTS
These dangerous bots have whirling blades that do a great deal of damage to anything they touch. To attack them, wait for the blades to stop and then use melee attacks. They're easily destroyed if you can get close enough. As with helibots, their hulls can be picked up and thrown. The hull is only around for a short time before exploding. Make sure Mr. Incredible isn't holding it over his head when it blows.

ROBOTS

Nomanisan Island is teeming with automated security forces. Here's a quick look at the robot foes you're up against.

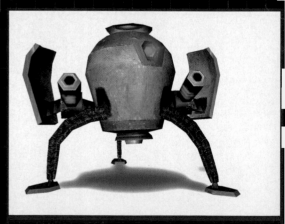

HELIBOTS
These flying robots aren't very tough, but they can be a problem for Mr. Incredible, who is the only member of the family who encounters them. They shoot electricity in a straight line across the ground; get out of its path when you hear it crackling. To destroy them, jump up and punch them or toss an object at them. Mr. Incredible can pick up their hulls and use them as projectiles, but they detonate shortly after the helibot is destroyed, so do it quickly.

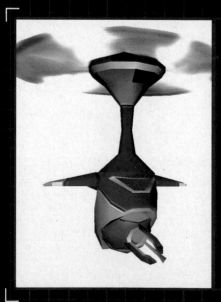

LEAPERBOTS
Leaperbots have a tremendously powerful guided missile system. They launch missiles into the air and then acquire a target. When you see the flashing red lines, that means your character has been acquired as a target. Jump out of the way. If you move quickly, the missiles land without doing any damage. Leaperbots jump out of range if you get too close. The only way to stop them is to chase them until they can't jump back anymore and then attack. Once you get close enough, they're easily demolished.

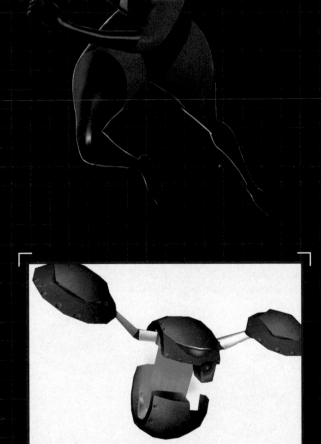

VELOCIBOTS
Velocibots are spinning, automated flying machines that fire lasers. They are very fast and fairly dangerous. Mr. Incredible faces them twice, but each time he has a weapon at his disposal—the first time he's riding a velocipod, the second time he has a turret. Simply shoot them to destroy them.

SEEKERBOTS
These flying robots fly straight into a character, detonating upon impact. They only appear in one level, and you have a turret with which to fire at them. They're not tough, but they're numerous.

BOSSES

TURRETS

Mounted guns are found throughout Nomanisan Island and Syndrome's base and laboratory. They do a good deal of damage, but they can be destroyed with a single hit.

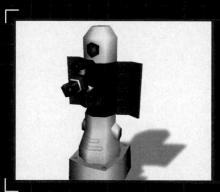

AUTOTURRETS
The more common of the two primary turrets, autoturrets fire lasers and can knock a character back. They take a moment to charge between each volley of shots, so attack them when they aren't firing. Throwing objects at them also destroys them.

NOTE
In later levels, you encounter some wall- and ceiling-mounted turrets. These behave exactly like autoturrets and can be eliminated with a single hit.

DOUBLE TURRETS
Much tougher than autoturrets, double turrets—as the name implies—have two mounted guns. But not only can they deal double the damage, they are also more resistant to damage and take a few hits to destroy. When a double turret is demolished, you can pick it up and fire its guns at enemies.

BOMB VOYAGE HELICOPTER
Bomb Voyage is the first boss you face in the game, and he's safely hiding in his helicopter. He isn't much of a problem, but his copter is armed to the blades with missiles and a laser gun. Wait for him to show his face, then pick up the bombs he lobs and throw them at the helicopter!

VIPER
The Viper is an aircraft with two horizontal propellers. It makes several appearances, but you only fight it once. It fires missiles, which can be shot out of the sky. When it attacks, the Viper is accompanied by seekerbots.

TANK

One of the deadliest foes in the game, the tank has a wide variety of devastating attacks. Its attacks follow a pattern; knowing it can help you avoid taking too much damage. Among its attacks is its ability to lob bombs. The only way to defeat it is to throw these bombs back at it. Mr. Incredible faces several tanks throughout the game, so learning how to beat them quickly and effectively proves crucial.

OMNIDROID

The only boss tougher than a tank is the Omnidroid. And the only boss tougher than an Omnidroid is a new and improved Omnidroid. Mr. Incredible fights three models of this robotic behemoth throughout the game, with each upgrade more deadly and powerful than the last.

BANK HEIST
CHAPTER 3

01. You begin standing on a rooftop, looking out at the skyline of the city. Bomb Voyage's henchmen are close by, so get moving quickly.
02. Turn around and jump over the nearby ducts.

BONUS ITEM

There's a bonus item on a raised platform near your starting point.

04. Continue forward and turn right onto the bridge connecting the two buildings. Your first fight is ahead.
05. Two henchmen wait on the bridge. At this point, use your standard punch to fight them.
06. Continue across the bridge to the other side. Grab the Incredi-Power icon power-up to learn about Incredi-Punches.
07. On the next rooftop you're besieged by a large group of henchmen. Use your Incredi-Punch to attack them.

MR. INCREDIBLE

Enemies: HENCHMEN, BOMB-TOSSING HENCHMEN, FLYING LOBBER HENCHMEN

Mr. Incredible must race across the rooftops to stop Bomb Voyage and his henchmen. This mission teaches you the basic action and combat controls.

TIP

Destroying ducts and other objects can often reveal hidden power-ups. If you've taken any damage, destroy the ducts next to the air-conditioning unit to find some health.

BONUS ITEM

There are health power-ups in three corners of the bank. In the fourth corner, to the right of the vault door, is a bonus item.

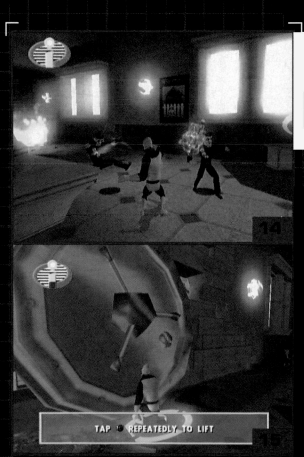

09. Go around the air-conditioning unit and run toward the searchlights. Another group of henchmen is just ahead. Attack them with a combination of Incredi-Punches and regular punches.
10. Turn left at the searchlights, and then go right onto the bridge. This bridge, which leads to the bank, has a health power-up. Grab it, then run forward into the bank.
11. The bank has already been attacked, and the entrance is ablaze. Be careful not to touch the flames.
12. Inside the bank, two large groups of henchmen attack, one group from each side. Fight them with Incredi-Punches.

14. Move to the other side of the bank and take out any remaining henchmen.
15. When the henchmen are defeated, run to the back of the bank. Stand near the vault door, which is lodged in the wall, and repeatedly press the throw button to lift the door and throw it clear.

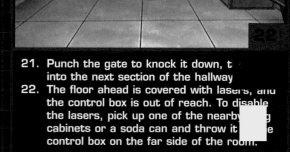

PRESS ◉ TO GRAB OBJECTS

21. Punch the gate to knock it down, t
    into the next section of the hallway

22. The floor ahead is covered with lasers, and
    the control box is out of reach. To disable
    the lasers, pick up one of the nearby   g
    cabinets or a soda can and throw it   e
    control box on the far side of the room.

16. Stand at the marker, then press and hold the jump button.
    This activates Mr. Incredible's Incredi-Jump. Release the button
    and Mr. Incredible springs off the nearby pole.

17. Mr. Incredible crashes down on a ledge opposite the
    bank, just in time to see Frozone fly by in hot pursuit of
    Bomb Voyage.

18. Two groups of henchmen will jump from the roof to attack
    Mr. Incredible. Attack them and move forward.

19. Run to the end of the ledge and enter the building through
    the destroyed wall.

20. Some lasers protect the area ahead. Attack the laser control
    box to disable it. The box is right next to the gate, marked
    with a lightning bolt.

CAUTION

Remember: Fire hurts Mr. Incredible! Avoid the flames as you enter the building.

THROW HENCHMEN AT THE CONTROL

PRESS ⊙ TO GRAB THE PIPE

23. Run to the gate and attack it to knock it out of the way.
24. Turn right and continue down the hall. Another gate blocks your path. Either punch it or throw a filing cabinet at it to clear the path.
25. A henchman will drop down from an opening in the ceiling in the next hallway section. Attack him and then destroy the next gate.
26. Another group of lasers blocks your path and another henchman will drop down and attack you. Grab him and throw him at the laser control box, which is to the right of the open gate ahead.
27. Continue forward and turn right at the end the hallway.

28. The floor has collapsed and tall flames prevent you from traveling any further. Jump through the nearby window onto the ledge.
29. Turn left and follow the ledge around to the marker.
30. Stand on the marker and jump to grab the pipe.

THE INCREDIBLES

TIP Mr. Incredible can pull enemies off of ledges by shimmying under them and pressing the Incredi-Punch button.

BONUS ITEM

Jump through the open window on the room's right side, then run forward on the ledge to find the third and final bonus item for this level.

PRESS ○ TO GRAB THE PIPE

31. Jump up again to grab the ledge, then pull yourself up onto the next roof.
32. Attack the henchman on the roof, then run forward. At the end of the ledge, drop down to the right.
33. Go forward and turn left. Continue around the roof to another pipe.
34. Jump up and grab the pipe, then jump up again to grab the ledge. Pull yourself onto the roof.
35. Two henchmen stand on the ledge. Knock one out and then grab his cohort.
36. Throw the henchman at the laser control box next to the window. If you've already attacked both henchmen, you can jump up and attack the box.
37. The box disables the lasers blocking the window. Jump through the window.
38. This control room is full of henchmen. Use your standard punch to take them out, and save your Incredi-Power until a large group surrounds you. Then use Mr. Incredible's jumping Incredi-Punch to take out the whole group.

40. Run toward the boarded window at the opposite end of the control room. As you approach, the window explodes and more henchmen appear. Attack them, then jump through the window.
41. Bomb Voyage appears and begins attacking with his helicopter. His initial attacks don't do much damage, but you're defenseless.

CAUTION

You can pick up the enemies' bombs only after they turn green. If you touch them while they are still red, they explode.

RUN TO THE NEXT SAFE AREA!

PULL AND HOLD THE RIGHT TRIGGER TO D

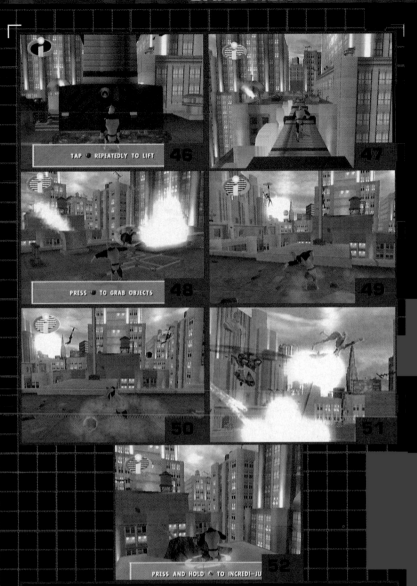

TAP ● REPEATEDLY TO LIFT

PRESS ● TO GRAB OBJECTS

PRESS AND HOLD ⌃ TO INCREDI-JU

42. Turn left and jump onto the nearby platform. Stand on the marker.
43. Jump up to grab the zip line. Mr. Incredible slides down to the next roof, picking up a health power-up along the way.
44. When he touches down, immediately take cover behind the nearby air-conditioning unit. The helicopter attacks again. Remember to crouch for maximum cover.
45. Move toward the helicopter, taking cover to avoid its fire. Work your way toward the tall sign at the roof's far end.

46. Stand on the marker at the base of the sign and repeatedly press the throw button.
47. Mr. Incredible knocks the sign over, creating a bridge to the next roof. Jump onto the sign and run across.
48. A group of lobber henchmen wait on the next roof. You have two options for defeating them . . . either run up and attack them hand to hand or pick up their bombs and throw them back.
49. When the lobber henchmen are defeated, the flying lobber henchmen arrive. They are in the air away from the building, out of range of your melee attack.
50. Grab their bombs and toss them back at them. Be careful . . . if you're hit by a bomb while holding one, both bombs explode.
51. After you defeat the flying lobber henchmen, Frozone again slides by, chasing the helicopter. As he passes, he knocks over a flagpole.
52. Walk up to the marker near the flagpole and press and hold the jump button. Release the jump button to perform an Incredi-Jump. Mr. Incredible sails through the air toward the large building opposite.

SKYLINE STRETCH
CHAPTER 4

MRS. INCREDIBLE

Enemies: HENCHMEN,
LOBBER HENCHMEN,
FLYING LOBBER HENCHMEN

Now it's Mrs. Incredible's turn to chase Bomb Voyage. She must use her fantastic elasticity to make her way across the roofs of the city and defeat his henchmen.

01. Mrs. Incredible begins facing a flagpole. Stretch out and grab it to swing across the gap.
02. When she reaches the highest point in her swing, release the pole to drop down on the roof ahead.
03. Two henchmen are on a platform ahead. Grab one of the henchmen and use him as a weapon against the other.
04. Two flying lobber henchmen ascend into view. Once again, use the "grab and throw" method to attack them.
05. Mrs. Incredible automatically grabs onto the police helicopter as it passes. It drops her off on another rooftop.

06. A posse of henchmen immediately approaches and attacks. Use Mrs. Incredible's standard attack to deal with them.

BONUS ITEM

Run toward the billboard on the roof. There is a small gap in the fence on the left side of the billboard.

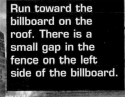

Jump onto the ledge of the roof and then onto the billboard. You find the first bonus item and a health power-up. Return to the roof through the gap in the fence.

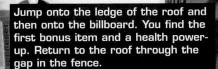

THROW THE HENCHMEN AT THE WAREHOU

09. Run to the Inredi-Power icon power-up. Grab it and drop onto the next roof.
10. Use Mrs. Incredible's Incredi-Punch to attack the henchmen.
11. Continue moving along the roof and grab the Incredi-Power icon power-up. Turn right to face the warehouse door.
12. Grab the henchman and throw them at the warehouse door.
13. Enter the warehouse. A small group of henchmen bounds around the corner. Attack them all from the entry area.

BONUS ITEM

Turn left at the entrance to the warehouse. The second bonus item is hidden among the shelves. Grab it before proceeding.

TIP

Remember that Mrs. Incredible can enter a first-person view to make targeting easier.

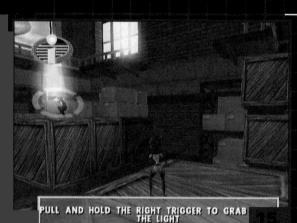

PULL AND HOLD THE RIGHT TRIGGER TO GRAB THE LIGHT

15. Run into the center of the warehouse and jump onto the crates. A lobber henchman appears on the taller crates ahead. Grab him and throw him, or pick up one of his bombs and toss it at him.
16. A lamp hangs over the taller crates. Use it to swing over the gap.
17. Turn to the left. A lobber henchman guards the tall shelves on the other side of the warehouse. Eliminate him before continuing forward.

19. Jump to the next crate. Target the lamp hanging over the shelves and swing over to them.
20. If you're hurt, there's a health power-up on the nearby crates. Jump up on the crates to grab it.
21. Run to the end of the shelves. A lobber henchman guards the tall stack of crates on the other side of the warehouse. Attack him.
22. Use the lamp hanging over these crates to haul yourself over.
23. Jump from the crates onto the small ledge. Run along the ledge to the gap. Use the nearby lamp to swing over the gap.
24. Jump through the demolished window out onto the roof. Bomb Voyage's helicopter is here, but the police helicopter attacks, chasing it off.

25. A group of flying lobber henchmen attacks Mrs. Incredible. Use the grab-and-throw method to hurl them at each other or pick up their bombs and toss them back.
26. When the last flying lobber henchman is defeated, the police helicopter appears. Grab onto it for a ride to the next roof.

27. The ground ahead is electrically charged and instantly knocks Mrs. Incredible out if she touches it. Use the lamps to swing over to safety.
28. Turn the corner. To proceed safely, you must knock out the air-conditioning unit. Grab the lobber henchmen who appear and toss them at the unit to destroy it. You need to hit it three times.
29. Jump over the air-conditioning unit and turn right. Follow the roof around to the next unit.
30. You can't proceed until the air-conditioning unit is destroyed. Grab the lobber henchmen and throw them at the unit.

BONUS ITEM

Jump over the air-conditioning unit and run forward to find the third and final bonus item between metal ducts.

CAUTION

Be careful of the helicopter's missiles. They do a great deal of damage. Stay moving to avoid being hit!

32. Jump through the gap in the fence to the roof below. There's another unsafe area, and another air-conditioning unit. Grab the henchmen who attack and throw them at the unit to disable the electricity.

33. Another electrical area blocks your path. Stand on the small ledge at the edge of the area and grab the flying lobber henchmen who appear from the gap ahead. Toss them at the air-conditioning unit to destroy it.

34. Jump over the unit to the ledge. Bomb Voyage's helicopter appears and knocks a support loose from the large sign. Use the support to swing across the gap.

35. There are two more electrical barriers. Grab the lamps hanging overhead to swing across the charged ground.

36. Once you clear the two charged areas, Bomb Voyage departs. The police helicopter appears. Grab the nearby health power-up, then grab onto the helicopter. It lifts you to the next roof.

37. Run around the corner. Grab and throw the flying lobber henchmen to destroy the air-conditioning unit.

38. Grab the health power-up in the corner, then run down the small alley.

39. A group of henchmen drops from the roof above. Take them out with a combination of Incredi-Punches and standard attacks.

40. Continue along the roof to the crane. Grab onto the crane; it hoists Mrs. Incredible up to the next roof.
41. Grab the health and the Incredi-Power icon power-ups near the water tower.
42. A large group of henchmen approaches from the opposite end of the roof. Grab and throw them at one another, and use Incredi-Punches if they surround Mrs. Incredible.
43. The next section is tricky. The entire area is electrically charged and there is no way to disable it. You must swing from lamp to lamp to make it safely across.
44. When swinging, wait until you target the next lamp, then let go of the lamp you're on and quickly grab onto the next. There are three lamps in total.

45. You can hang on to your current lamp in relative safety until the next is in reach. Flying lobber henchmen shoot bombs at you, but your constant motion makes them less of a threat.
46. Mrs. Incredible runs ahead to complete the level where a police helicoptor takes off in pursuit of Bomb Voyage.

BUDDY AND BOMB VOYAGE

CHAPTER 5

MR. INCREDIBLE

Enemy: BOMB VOYAGE

Buddy is giving Mr. Incredible a lift, but it's a wild ride. Mr. Incredible must avoid the obstacles in the path if he wants to survive long enough to confront Bomb Voyage.

01. Mr. Incredible has grabbed onto Buddy and is being carried over the city. Unfortunately, the extra weight is pulling Buddy down.
02. After takeoff, Buddy turns right down a street. Quickly swing to the left to avoid the cable. Another cable comes up. Swing right to avoid it.
03. To avoid the third cable on the street, swing to the left.
04. Buddy flies higher and turns left. Quickly swing right to avoid the first cable on this stretch of the flight, then swing left to avoid the second.
05. Buddy heads down, but three more cables block the way. Swiftly swing left, then right, then left again.

06. After Buddy makes the next right turn, swing right and then left.
07. Finally, Buddy reaches a clear section of street...clear except for Bomb Voyage, that is. Swing around to avoid his missiles.

BONUS ITEM

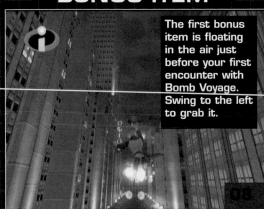

The first bonus item is floating in the air just before your first encounter with Bomb Voyage. Swing to the left to grab it.

09. Buddy flies down another clear street, then turns left. Immediately swing to the right to avoid the first cable.
10. This stretch of road has two more cables. Swing left and then left again to avoid them.
11. Buddy descends down to street level, almost hitting another cable on the way.
12. Mr. Incredible is in the way of oncoming traffic! Swing either right or left to avoid the cars.
13. Buddy ascends and turns left. Quickly swing to the right to avoid the first cable.

14. Swing left and then left again to avoid the next two cables. There's one more cable on this stretch; swing right to avoid it.
15. Bomb Voyage appears yet again. Swing to avoid his missiles.
16. Buddy turns right and then left, heading straight for a cable. Swing left to avoid it.
17. Two more cables ahead: Swing right and then right again to stay clear of them.

BONUS ITEM

The second cable of this last pair is the final obstacle of the flight. When you swing right to avoid it, you also grab the second bonus item.

19. Buddy drops Mr. Incredible on a rooftop and the final battle with Bomb Voyage begins.
20. To defeat Bomb Voyage, you must pick up the bombs he tosses and throw them at the helicopter. After you successfully damage the helicopter, Bomb Voyage resorts to one of two attacks.
21. His first and less dangerous, weapon is a machine gun. You can easily dodge the shots by running away from the helicopter and jumping when the shots are about to hit.

22. Bomb Voyage also attacks with missiles. These are much more dangerous than the machine gun and they are guided as well, making them difficult to dodge.
23. When you see a missile approaching, crouch down. As soon as the missile is near, roll to the left or right to avoid it. The roll happens too fast for the missile to reacquire the target, so it explodes harmlessly behind Mr. Incredible.
24. Use these techniques to avoid Bomb Voyage's attacks until he begins throwing bombs again. Then repeat the process. You must hit him with six bombs total to bring him down.

TIP

Health power-ups are hidden in the objects on the roof. Bomb Voyage's attacks will most likely reveal them, but you can punch a few ducts to find some health if you're taking too much damage.

BONUS ITEM

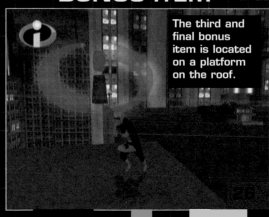

The third and final bonus item is located on a platform on the roof.

APARTMENT INFERNO

CHAPTER 6

01. Run forward through the hallway. A beam overhead collapses, but it does not hit Mr. Incredible.
02. Two arsonists wait at the base of the stairs. Jump over them and attack from behind.

! CAUTION

To attack arsonists, either get behind them or throw something at them. Don't attack from the front.

MR. INCREDIBLE

Enemies: ARSONISTS

Mr. Incredible must catch up to Frozone and escape the burning building. It won't be easy, though . . . the place has been overrun with arsonists, and the walls are literally collapsing around him.

03. Run up the stairs after both arsonists have been defeated.
04. Frozone is standing at the top. He tells Mr. Incredible that he's going to look for civilians.
05. The stairs have collapsed. Run to the small outcropping on the left side and jump over the gap.
06. Turn right down the hallway. The ceiling caves in, preventing any further progress in that direction.

07. Turn left and run up the stairs. These, too, have collapsed. Jump to the railing on the left, then jump forward to reach the top.
08. Turn left and stand on the marker. Grab and lift the broken wall to clear a path.
09. Just past the wall, some fallen beams block the hallway. Punch them to knock them out of the way.

10. When you reach the first large room, Frozone appears on the opposite side. He's found one occupant, and is going to look for more.
11. Run into the room and grab the nearby health power-up, if needed. Turn left and run along what remains of the floor.
12. Two arsonists jump down and block Mr. Incredible's path. Pick up the furniture and throw it at them.
13. Move forward and turn right. Two jets of flame are in the path. Jump over the first.

TIP Mr. Incredible can roll in any direction by holding a direction and pressing jump while crouching.

14. To safely dodge the second flame jet, crouch and then roll forward.
15. More arsonists wait past the flame jets. There's plenty of room to hop over them and attack and you can also use some pieces of debris as projectiles.
16. Turn right at the broken wall and proceed to the pillar. Grab the health power-up if needed. Stand on the marker and lift the pillar to create a bridge across the floor.

BONUS ITEM

Look to your left at the first pillar . . . there's a bonus item behind the broken wall.

18. Jump onto the pillar and run across the gap. There's a health power-up behind the debris to the right, and an Incredi-Power icon to the left.
19. Two arsonists wait on the next set of steps. There's nothing to throw nearby, so you need to jump over them and attack.
20. Turn right at the end of the hall, sticking close to the right wall to avoid the flame jet.

BONUS ITEM

The second bonus item is on top of the fireplace, to your right as you finish crossing the third pillar. Use the nearby debris to jump up to it.

21. The next hall is very treacherous; there are two flame jets and an arsonist. Wait until the first jet has stopped, then jump over the arsonist and attack him from behind.
22. Run past the second jet when it turns off. As you approach the end of the hall, a beam falls and two more jets erupt around it. Run under the beam when the lower jet is off. Grab the health power-up at the end of the hall.
23. You enter another large room. Turn left and run toward the stairs. Frozone appears again, with another civilian in tow.
24. Two arsonists run up the stairs. Jump over them and attack.
25. Turn right at the bottom of the stairs and run to the next pillar. Stand on the marker and lift the pillar; it falls on the arsonist blocking your path.
26. Run across the pillar to the next section of floor. Turn left and move to the next pillar. Again, stand on the marker and lift. When the pillar falls, jump onto it and run across the gap.
27. Turn right and run to the marker near the third pillar. Lift it until it falls, then run across to the far side of the room.
28. Two arsonists attack when you jump off the pillar. Wait until they stop firing their flamethrowers, then attack.

30. Run up the steps and grab the Incredi-Power icon as you turn the corner into the next hallway. A section of the floor falls away and flames shoot up from below. Jump over the hole.
31. Turn right and start up the stairs. They collapse. Jump and grab the swinging lamp. Swing forward and release the lamp. You land safely on the landing.

TAP ⊙ REPEATEDLY TO TILT

32. The hallway ahead is in bad shape. Jump over the gap onto the next section of floor.
33. The floor begins to teeter-totter. Wait until the far side has risen to its highest point, then begin running forward.

BONUS ITEM

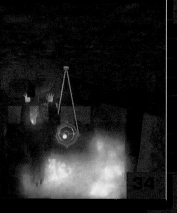

The third bonus item is above the far end of the teeter-tottering floor. To grab it, run to the left side of the far end when it is at its highest point, then crouch and jump.

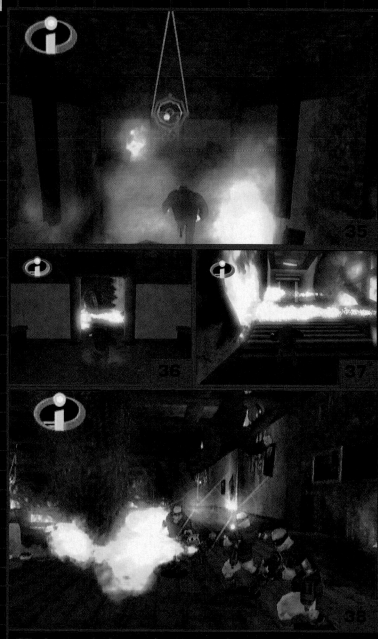

35. Jump to the lamp and swing over the next gap. Release the lamp and run forward to grab the Incredi-Power icon.
36. A flame jet blocks passage through the next doorway. Wait until it shuts off, then run forward. Turn right and run up the stairs.
37. Continue up the stairs. You come to a pair of flame jets, which shut off for very short intervals. Stay to the left, then rush forward as soon as the coast is clear. Repeat this with the second jet.
38. Go through the doorway and up the sloping hallway to the next large room. Three arsonists attack as soon as you enter. You should have some Incredi-Power saved up, so use a jumping Incredi-Punch to knock them all out.

39. Grab the nearby health power-up and then run toward the swinging lamp. Jump and grab it to swing across the gap.

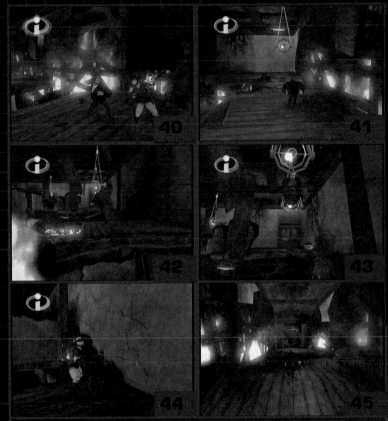

40. Two arsonists are waiting on the next platform. You land behind one of them. Immediately attack him, and then turn and jump over the second to attack him from behind.
41. Jump across the gap. Run forward, jump to the lamp, and swing across the next gap.
42. Turn left at the corner. The floor collapses below you, so quickly jump to the platform ahead.
43. Two swinging lamps hang over the next gap. Jump to the first and swing forward to its highest point. Jump to the second lamp and swing to the floor ahead.
44. Two arsonists immediately attack Mr. Incredible. Attack them both, then go through the nearby doorway.
45. Run down the burning hallway to the doorway at the far end. Frozone appears with the residents he rescued, and everyone escapes safely. Everyone except the arsonists, that is.

LATE FOR SCHOOL

CHAPTER 7

01. You have five minutes to guide Dash to school. The first section is fairly easy, but it gets increasingly complicated. Hitting small obstacles trips Dash up; hitting large obstacles sends him back to the previous checkpoint.

02. Stay on the right side of the road to avoid the oncoming cars.

03. The first major obstacle comes at the 9 percent mark. Vee left to avoid the car in the intersection. Then turn right imn diately to avoid the car ahead.

DASH

Enemies: NONE

Dash has missed the bus. Help him get to school before the bell rings at 8:00!

CAUTION

If you find yourself headed toward a manhole with no time to turn, jump over it. Manholes trip Dash, costing him precious seconds.

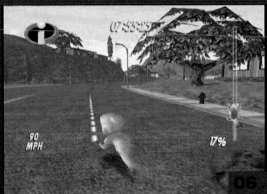

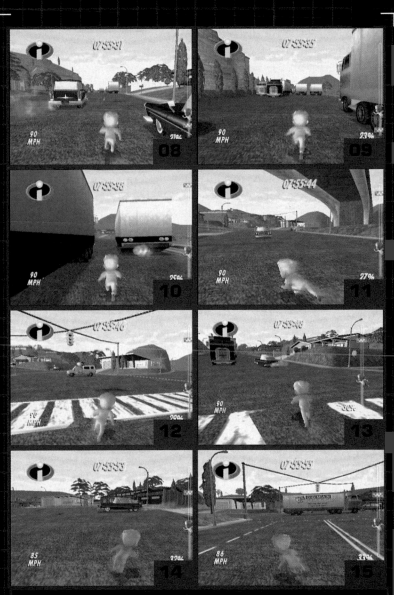

08. After the checkpoint, you have a brief section of light traffic. Run between the cars on the right side of the road.
09. As you approach the bend, you see a large group of trucks headed in both directions on the road.
10. Stay to the right and run between the two trucks.
11. Watch out for the green car headed in your direction as you pass under the bridge. Either keep right or make a hard left to avoid it.
12. In the next intersection, a small truck is turning toward you. Move right to dodge it.
13. Almost immediately, a purple car turns right onto the road. Move to the far right side and pass it.
14. Another car speeds on to the road from the right. Move quickly right, so you don't slam into the side.
15. Be very careful in the busy intersection ahead. Veer left to avoid the truck.

05. At the 16 percent mark, make a hard left to avoid the car and the truck.
06. Use Dash's Incredi-Boost power when the road is clear.
07. The first checkpoint is at the 20 percent mark.

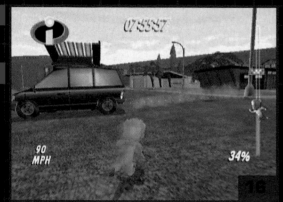

16. In the intersection, make a hard right around the oncoming cars and into the clear lanes.

17. You see construction ahead. Move to the far left side of the road to avoid the blockades and the approaching vehicle.

18. Stay on the left side of the road as you approach the train tracks.

19. Jump through the gap in the train's cargo beds to safely reach the opposite side of the tracks. The second checkpoint is just past the train.

20. Move left to avoid the green car and the police cruiser following it in hot pursuit.

21. After the police chase, move to the far right side of the road to dodge the blue car backing out of its driveway.

22. Stay on the right side to avoid the next car and the construction area as well.

23. Past the construction area, a third car backs out of a driveway. Keep to the right side.

24. At the 46 percent mark, a small car bolts into the road. Stay to the right to avoid both it and another car coming up the road on the left.

25. Run straight for the gravel pile when it comes into view.

26. Jump off the gravel pile to clear the exposed pipes and the barricades.

BONUS ITEM

You can grab the first bonus item near the gravel ramp just before the tunnel entrance. Jump off the left side of the ramp—the bonus item is hanging in the air over the pipes.

27. At the 50 percent mark, head left to dodge the oncoming car and avoid the construction area to the right.
28. Veer right between the construction areas.
29. After passing the second construction area, turn left and jump over the manhole to reach the left lanes.
30. Use the gravel pile to jump over the exposed pipes ahead.

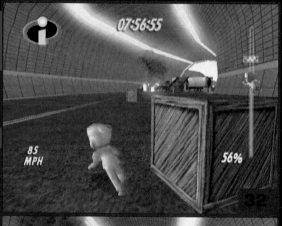

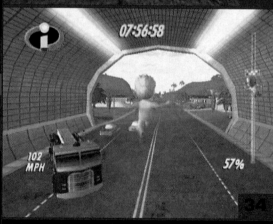

32. Stay on the right side of the road when you enter the tunnel, but avoid the boxes scattered about.
33. As you approach the accident, aim for the truck ramp. Use Incredi-Boost to accelerate as you ascend the ramp.
34. Jump from the top of the ramp over the truck ahead. Quickly move to the right to avoid the cars in the left lane.

35. Slow down as you approach the next intersection. It's extremely busy and charging straight into it means certain tardiness.
36. Stay in the dead center of the road. The trucks pass, leaving a small window of opportunity. Use Incredi-Boost to shoot through the gap. The third checkpoint is on the other side.
37. Get into the right lane to avoid the construction area and the red car ahead.
38. Quickly move left through the gap between the red car and the green car parked in the right lane.
39. Run toward the truck ramp at the blocked intersection. Use Incredi-Boost on the ramp to jump over the truck.

BONUS ITEM

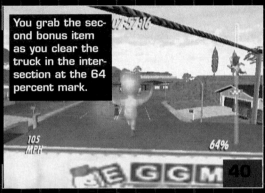

You grab the second bonus item as you clear the truck in the intersection at the 64 percent mark.

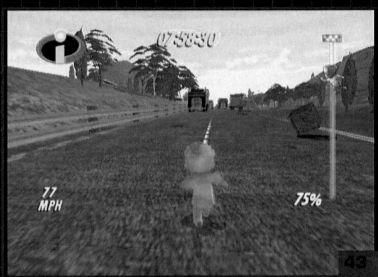

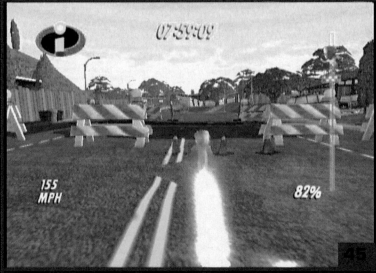

41. There's traffic in both directions, so stay close to the center line to easily dodge the cars on the left and right.
42. There's another busy intersection at the 69 percent mark; stay to the center of the road to avoid the traffic.

43. As you climb the hill, stay to the left and dodge the boxes falling out of the truck ahead. The truck to the right makes it too difficult to dodge easily on that side.
44. When the right lane is clear, move right. Continue dodging the boxes as they fall. The fourth checkpoint is at the top of the hill.
45. After the turn, aim for the gap in the barricades, use Incredi-Boost, and jump over the exposed pipes.

46. Move to the right lane and avoid the construction area to the left.
47. Veer left between the construction areas and jump over the manhole in the intersection.
48. Immediately move back to the right to avoid the next construction zone.
49. Keep to the far right and use Incredi-Boost to move past the truck as it backs into the driveway, then immediately shoot left to avoid the parked car just ahead.
50. There's a truck with a ramp stopped at the busy intersection ahead. Use Incredi-Boost up the ramp.

51. Jump off the top of the ramp to sail high above the intersection.

BONUS ITEM

After clearing the final intersection, quickly move to the right lane to grab the third bonus item, located at the 97 percent mark. Make sure to avoid the bus ahead!

53. After you've cleared the intersection, the school is in sight. Use one last Incredi-Boost to speed over the final stretch of road.

BEACH LANDING
CHAPTER 8

MR. INCREDIBLE

Enemies: AUTOTURRETS, HELIBOTS, BLADEBOTS

Summoned by Mirage, Mr. Incredible arrives on the remote island of Nomanisan for a top-secret assignment. Little does he know the menacing army of robotic enemies that stand in his way are all compliments of the evil genius Syndrome. Mr. Incredible must hunt down the largest robot of them all, the Omnidroid, but there are hordes of enemies that stand in his way.

01. Run forward until Mirage tells you about the autoturrets. She tells you to take cover until they begin to recharge, at which point you can run forward and attack.
02. Mirage's advice is helpful, but there isn't always cover. A better strategy is to throw a crate at the autoturret before it begins shooting. Pick up a crate and throw it at the first autoturret.
03. Two more autoturrets pop out of the ground ahead. Destroy them both.
04. Another pair of autoturrets guards the next section of jungle, one on each side of the path. Once again, use crates to take them both out.
05. The first helibot is guarding the path past these autoturrets. To eliminate it, either throw a crate or jump up and attack it in the air.

TIP

If you fall into the water at any point in the first section of the beach, you can climb back up using the bars on the nearby cliff.

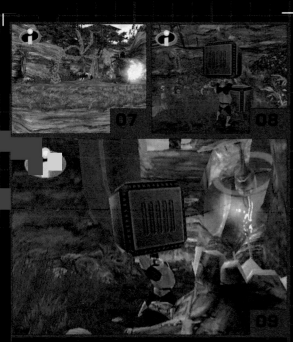

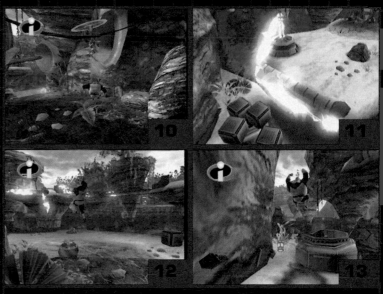

10. Two more helibots stand in your way. Destroy them both before jumping down to the beach.
11. As you approach the beach, you see that the bar you need to jump to is electrically charged. The charge is sporadic.
12. Jump down to the beach to meet your first bladebot. Mirage gives you a quick debriefing on their behavior: Avoid them when the blades are active, then attack as they recharge.
13. To stop bladebots from being created, you must disable the robot generator. Use a jumping attack to destroy it.

07. Grab the health power-up, then stand on the mark and grab hold of the tree. Mr. Incredible uses the tree to catapult himself to the next cliff.
08. Use the crates to destroy the two autoturrets guarding the path below.
09. Jump down and turn right. A helibot is hovering above the path. Destroy it with a crate or with a jumping attack.

TIP

If you're hurt, you can find a health power-up on the right side of the beach, behind some crates.

TIP

When you destroy a helibot, you can pick up its hull and use it as a projectile!

BONUS ITEM

To find the first bonus item, take a little detour after the second bridge.

24. Turn left after crossing the bridge. Jump to the small platform sticking out from the cliff. Remember: The longer you hold jump, the farther Mr. Incredible leaps.
25. Run across the platform and drop to the small area below. Continue forward, then jump across the gap and attack the autoturret.
26. Run to the far end of this outcropping and leap across toward the second autoturret. Destroy the autoturret, then attack the helibot.
27. Turn left and run toward the waterfall.
28. The bonus item is in the cave behind the waterfall.
29. Return to the main area by jumping up the steps near the second autoturret's former position.

30. Stand under the left cable and jump up to grab it. Mr. Incredible slides down the cable.
31. As you approach the overhanging rock, leap to the right cable to avoid being knocked down into the water. When you grab the right cable, you get an Incredi-Power icon.
32. Run forward, grab the health power-up, and destroy the bladebot and the robot generator.

TAP ● REPEATEDLY TO LIFT. PRESS ⋀ TO D

PRESS ● TO RELEASE CRANE

33. Jump up to the platform and destroy the autoturret. Leap across the gap to the next platform.

34. Watch for the helibot that emerges from the tube! Wait until it is over the platform, then jump up and destroy it.

35. Stand on the marker and lift the pillar. It falls, creating a bridge across the water. Jump onto the pillar and run across.

36. Turn left through the small valley. Two autoturrets and a helibot guard the path. Quickly destroy all three with a series of Incredi-Punches and a jumping attack.

37. The bars on the wall ahead are electrified. You can't disable the electricity, so you have to time your climbing.

38. Jump to the first bar when the electricity is off. Then listen carefully. When the crackling of the electricity above stops, quickly jump up and grab the second bar. Jump from the bar to the cliff on your left, grabbing the Incredi-Power icon as you land.

39. Grab the crane and turn it so that it's hanging in the center of the gap between the two cliffs.

40. Jump to the crane and swing across the chasm. Release at the highest point of the swing to land on the cliff ahead.

41. Four autoturrets guard the cliff. Quickly attack them, because there is nowhere to take cover. Grab the health power-up near the autoturret on the lower right.
42. There's a helibot on the upper area of the cliff. Watch out for its electrical attack, then jump and destroy it when it recharges.

NOTE

At the top of the cliff, you see an Incredi-Power icon and a small metal platform. Step onto the platform to activate an elevator to the beach below. If you happen to fall during the next section, this elevator brings you back up to this point.

PRESS ⓧ TO RELEASE CRANE

PRESS ⓧ TO RELEASE DEVICE

44. Grab the crane and turn it so that the arm is hanging over the gap between the cliffs.
45. Jump to the crane and swing across the gap. The next cliff is heavily guarded, so be ready for combat.
46. Two autoturrets, a robot generator, and a helibot occupy the next cliff. Quickly attack the autoturrets, then jump and attack the helibot.

47. Grab the health power-up near the robot generator and then use a jumping Incredi-Punch to destroy the generator. Finish off any bladebots that have been produced.
48. Stand on the marker and grab the tree. Mr. Incredible launches himself to the next cliff.
49. Stand under the bar and wait for a pause in the electrical charge. Jump up and grab the bar, then jump to the next level.
50. Attack the two autoturrets and the helibot guarding the cliff, then grab the device.
51. Turn the device. This briefly disables the electricity on the cables nearby.

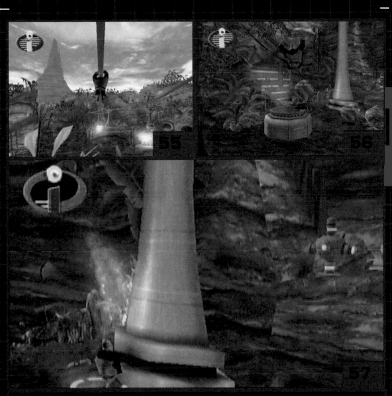

55. Jump up to the left cable and slide down. Leap to the right cable to avoid the helibot hovering in your way.
56. Run down the small dirt path. As you approach the security lasers, the robot generator releases two bladebots. Destroy the generator and the bots.
57. Stand on the marker at the base of the pillar. Lift the pillar to drop it across the gap. It falls and destroys the generator, disabling the security lasers.

BONUS ITEM

The second bonus item is on the cliff with the security laser generator. Run across the pillar to grab it. You can also find a health power-up here.

52. Stand on the marker and grab the tree, then release it to catapult back to the cliff. You must be fairly quick about it—the electricity is off only for a short time.
53. Stand under either of the cables and jump up to grab it. Slide down to the next cliff.
54. Destroy the generator to disable the electricity running through the cables. Grab the nearby Incredi-Power icon.

59. When the security lasers are disabled, enter the canyon. Grab the Incredi-Power icon as you turn right.
60. The canyon is heavily guarded. One autoturret is just ahead with two more immediately behind it. Use a jumping Incredi-Punch to take out the first autoturret, then run up and attack the others.
61. Two more autoturrets are installed just around the bend. Take them out with a jumping Incredi-Punch.
62. Run forward into the lagoon. Take a quick look around to get your bearings. Security lasers surround a pillar on the far side of the lagoon and there's a small island to the right. Jump over to this island.

63. When you reach the island, helibots attack, and three autoturrets pop up on the raised island across the lagoon.
64. Use jumping punches to destroy the helibots, then pick up their hulls and toss them at the autoturrets across the way.
65. When all three autoturrets are eliminated, repeat the procedure with the generators. Destroying the generators shuts off the security lasers.

TIP

If you need health while fighting in the lagoon, destroy the crate on the island. Inside, you will find a health power-up. There is another health power-up on the small island near the security lasers.

BONUS ITEM

TAP ⬤ REPEATEDLY TO LIFT. PRESS ⬆ TO   66

66. Jump to the small island, and then to the island with the pillar. Stand on the marker and lift the pillar to create a bridge. Jump onto the pillar and run across to the raised island.

The third bonus item is hidden among some crates on a small island near the entrance to the lagoon. To get it, run across the raised island to the far end and jump to the small island.

68 Find the marker near the tree on the raised island. Stand on the marker and grab the tree. Mr. Incredible launches himself over the monorail and into the center of Nomanisan Island.

NOMANISAN ISLAND

CHAPTER 9

01. After Mr. Incredible lands in the jungle, Omnidroid makes a brief appearance.
02. Run forward into the jungle. Ahead, you see a robot generator, a device, and an Incredi-Power icon.
03. As you approach, security lasers are activated. The robot generator has already released three bladebots, so destroy it before more appear. Then attack the bladebots.

MR. INCREDIBLE

Enemies: AUTOTURRETS, HELIBOTS, BLADEBOTS, LEAPERBOTS, SEEKERBOTS, DOUBLE TURRETS, VIPER

Mr. Incredible must continue his hunt for the Omnidroid through the dense jungle of Nomanisan Island. The island security devices are more numerous as he approaches the heart of the jungle.

BONUS ITEMS

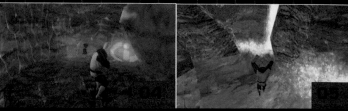

04. The first bonus item is right at the beginning of the level. Jump into the pool and swim under the first waterfall.
05. In the small grotto, you find the second bonus item and an Incredi-Power icon.

06. Grab the device and turn it to temporarily disable the security lasers.
07. Release the device and run toward the gate. Two autoturrets attack. Destroy them both, or simply run past them through the gate.
08. Turn left inside the gate to grab an Incredi-Power icon. You can destroy the generator if you want to permanently disable the security lasers you just passed through.

09. Two more autoturrets guard the path. Use standard attacks to take them out or pick up any of the rusted bladebot hulls lying around and use them as projectiles.
10. Run forward and turn right at the bend. Two more bladebots and an autoturret attack Mr. Incredible. Get close to the autoturrets and use a jumping Incredi-Punch to destroy the whole lot of them or run back and grab more bladebot hulls to attack from a distance.
11. A single autoturret sits in the center of the path ahead. Run up and punch it before it has a chance to fire.
12. As Mr. Incredible approaches the next clearing, more security lasers are activated.

PRESS ⦿ TO RELEASE DEVICE

13. There are several bladebots already deployed here, as well as two autoturrets near the gate. You can also find an Incredi-Power icon and a health power-up near the entrance to the clearing.
14. Destroy the bladebots and the autoturrets using jumping Incredi-Punches and standard attacks.
15. Turn right at the gate and jump over the tree stumps to find the robot generator. Destroy it, then grab the health power-up floating above.

16. When all the bots have been defeated, grab the device and turn it to disable the security field.
17. Quickly move over to the marker at the base of the gate. Lift the gate to rip it out and toss it out of the way.
18. Run through the gate before the lasers reactivate. Pick up one of the nearby bladebot hulls and throw it at the helibot.
19. There are two robot generators in the clearing. Destroy them both before engaging the bladebots themselves.
20. Attack the bladebots and the helibot. Once you've finished off the security forces, you can destroy the generator near the gate to disable the security lasers behind you.

NOTE

You can permanently disable every security laser field. It isn't necessary, but it's helpful if you need to go back and pick up power-ups.

CAUTION

Beware of the leaperbot missiles! When you see the red targeting indicator, quickly move out of the way.

PRESS ⬤ TO RELEASE DEVICE

TAP ⬤ REPEATEDLY TO LIFT

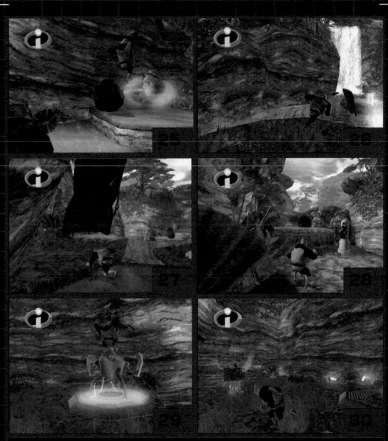

21. Grab the device and turn it to temporarily disable the next set of security lasers. Grab the health power-up near the device when you're done.
22. Run up the marker near the gate and grab and lift. The gate is torn away and thrown high into the air.
23. Through the gate, you encounter your first leaperbot. It immediately leaps back to its next roost. Run up and grab the health power-up if needed.

25. If you get hit with the leaperbots' missiles, grab the health power-up on the steps near the water.
26. Jump to the small island ahead. As you run forward, the leaperbot jumps to its next roost. Jump over the water to the next island and destroy the autoturret.
27. Jump to the rock outcropping. Watch out for the door! Those gates Mr. Incredible threw into the air had to land somewhere—unfortunately they're in his path.
28. Go around the door and attack the autoturret. The leaperbot fires more missiles your way, so keep moving.
29. Destroy the autoturret on the next level, then use a jumping Incredi-Punch to take out the leaperbot.
30. Turn left and attack the two autoturrets guarding the steps.

BONUS ITEM

PRESS ⊕ TO RELEASE DEV

Before heading up the steps to the next area, go back to the very beginning of this area.

31. Jump into the water and swim back to the small island near the first waterfall.
32. Jump to the small rock outcropping, then run into the cave behind the waterfall.
33. Grab the device and turn it. It doesn't turn off the lasers, but it does change their status.
34. Crouch and roll forward under the laser fields.
35. There are five laser fields to get by. Behind the fourth are an autoturret and the bonus item. Roll under the field, destroy the autoturret, and grab the bonus item.
36. Roll under the final laser field, then jump through the second waterfall, back into the lagoon.

37. When the leaperbot is destroyed and you have the bonus item, jump up the steps near the leaperbot's final roost.
38. Grab the health power-up at the top of the cliff, then run to the marker and grab the tree. Mr. Incredible catapults himself across the water.
39. You need to destroy the tower before proceeding. Jump down the hill and stand on the marker. Mr. Incredible lifts the huge piece of debris and flings it across the water at the tower.

PRESS AND HOLD ✧ TO GRAB ANTEN

40. Some damage was done, but the tower is still operational. Helibots come flying in. Attack the bots and use their hulls as projectiles against the tower.
41. Hit it with two helibot hulls and the tower is demolished. The antenna from the tower flies across the water and slams into the ground like a huge javelin.
42. Grab the antenna and use it to launch Mr. Incredible over the water.
43. A second leaperbot lurks nearby. It leaps back and fires some missiles, destroying the path over the water.

PRESS ● TO RELEASE CRANE

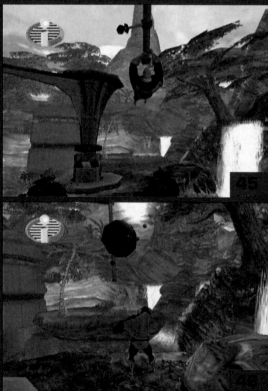

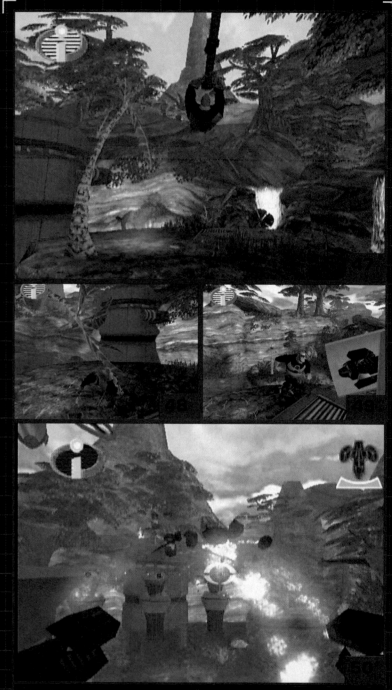

44. Run forward and grab the crane. Rotate it so that the arm is hanging between the two islands.
45. Jump to the crane and swing to the next island.
46. Grab a bladebot hull and throw it at the leaperbot to eliminate it. Otherwise, its missiles prevent you from using the next crane.

47. Grab the next crane and rotate it into position, then use it to swing across the next island.
48. Stand on the marker and grab the tree. Release the tree, and Mr. Incredible shoots up to the double turret platform.
49. Use an Incredi-Punch to destroy the double turret before it has a chance to fire at Mr. Incredible.
50. Pick up the turret. The towers across the water are launching seekerbots, and the viper is launching missiles. Concentrate on the towers first, but hit any missiles that come into range.

55. Stand on the marker and grab the antenna. Release it to launch Mr. Incredible to the cliff next to the tower. The exit is just ahead.

BONUS ITEM

Before leaving the level, turn right at the tower. The final bonus item is on the second destroyed tower. Jump across the towers to grab it.

51. Keep the turret aimed at the level of the towers, hitting the seekerbots as they cross your field of aim. Fire at the towers when there's a short break in the action.
52. When all three towers are destroyed, no more seekerbots are launched. Turn your attention to the viper.
53. Hit any missiles it fires, but keep your fire concentrated on the viper itself. It won't take much time to destroy it.
54. Release the turret, turn left, and jump over the small gap. Grab the nearby health power-up. Destroy the robot generator and any bladebots that have been released.

57 Run into the jungle to exit the level. Mr. Incredible comes face-to-serial number with the Omnidroid, which tosses him into a volcano!

VOLCANIC ERUPTION
CHAPTER 10

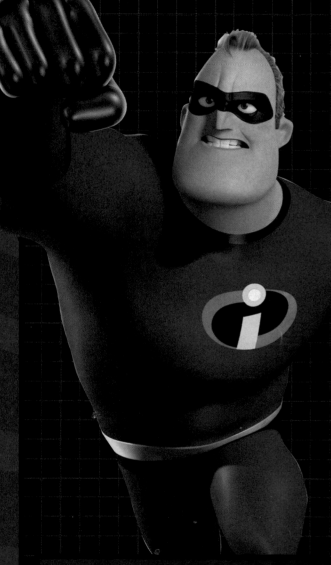

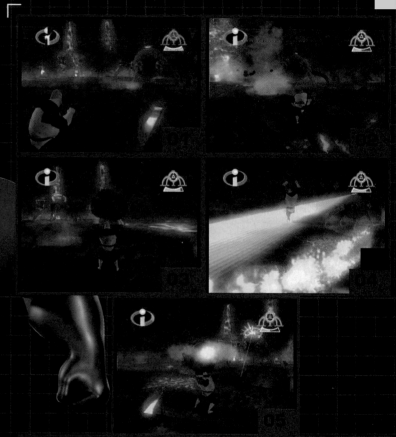

MR. INCREDIBLE

Enemy: OMNIDROID 08
Mr. Incredible must defeat the powerful Omnidroid 08. This is three rounds of rough, man vs. machine combat, all set in the heart of a volcano!

01. The Omnidroid is a very tough foe. He has an arsenal of different attacks, and each can do a good deal of damage to Mr. Incredible, so learn how to avoid each one.

02. His first attack is the least problematic. The Omnidroid digs up huge chunks of the volcano and slams them down on the ground. To avoid this attack, steer clear of the Omnidroid when it starts digging into the ground.

03. This attack is actually beneficial to Mr. Incredible. The chunks of volcano leave large rocks around. Pick up the rocks and throw them at the Omnidroid to damage it.

04. Its second attack is a bit trickier to dodge. The Omnidroid has a laser turret at its top. The laser creates a streak of fire in its path, so you must be sure to avoid both the laser and its aftermath. Jump over the laser, or run toward the Omnidroid as it fires. If you're right next to the Omnidroid, the laser won't hit you.

05. Another way to avoid the laser attack is to stop it before it starts. Throw a rock at the turret when it's charging, and the laser attack is aborted. This also does a good amount of damage to the Omnidroid.

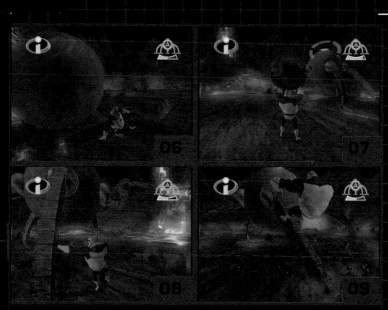

06. In what is perhaps the most devastating of its initial attacks, the Omnidroid retracts its arms and begins rolling at Mr. Incredible. Crouch, and then roll out of the way at the very last moment to avoid being steamrollered.
07. After the Omnidroid uses its ball attack, quickly find a rock. As soon as it assumes its standard form, throw the rock at its turret.
08. If you don't have quick access to a rock, run in and pummel the Omnidroid's legs. Use Incredi-Punches liberally.
09. Be careful when approaching the Omnidroid. It swipes at Mr. Incredible, knocking him back.

11. When the Omnidroid has taken a fair amount of damage, it leaps back to the cliffs across the lava, making melee attacks impossible.
12. The Omnidroid begins hurling rocks at Mr. Incredible. Pick up the rocks and hurl them back!

TIP

The rocks aren't just weapons. They also contain Incredi-Power icons and health power-ups. If Mr. Incredible is hurt, destroy some rocks with Incredi-Punches to replenish his health and Incredi-Power.

TIP

If Mr. Incredible is hurt, spend some time destroying rocks and collecting health while the Omnidroid is out of melee range. You can avoid its projectiles and get Mr. Incredible back into fighting shape.

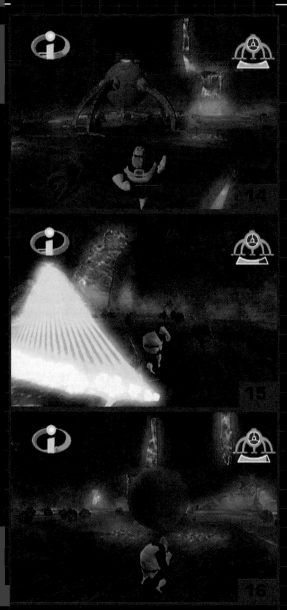

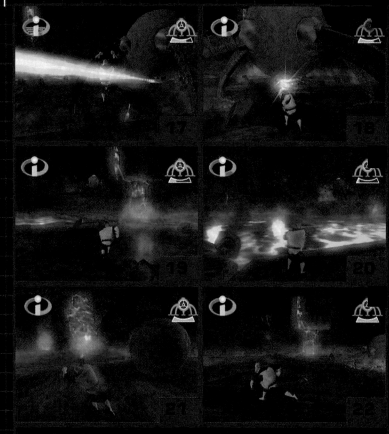

14. The battle isn't over yet. You need to go three rounds with the Omnidroid before it is destroyed.
15. In the second round, all of the Omnidroid's attacks are doubled. It fires its laser twice, and makes two passes as the ball.
16. It also has a new attack—a laser that fires from under its hull. Unlike the top laser, this fires several shots.

17. To avoid the lower laser, run and jump around the Omnidroid, circling in on its hull.
18. Run under the hull and hit the lower turret to do some serious damage to the Omnidroid.
19. When it has taken enough damage, the Omnidroid once again retreats to the cliffs and throw rocks at Mr. Incredible.
20. Pick up the rocks and throw them at the Omnidroid.
21. The third round is the toughest yet. The Omnidroid uses each attack three times, so be on guard—especially from the ball attack.
22. There's a new addition to its arsenal. During the third round, the Omnidroid extends its arms and spins across the ground. Run, jump, and roll as fast as you can to keep ahead of the whirling arms.

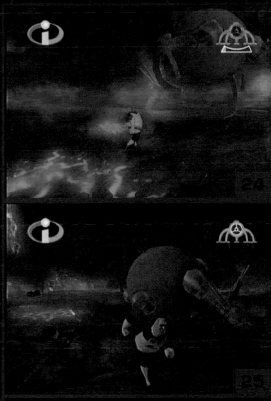

24. Keep attacking with both punches to its legs and lower turret, and by throwing rocks at the upper turret. Take breaks to look for health if needed, but getting the fight over quickly should be your main priority.
25. The Omnidroid stays in melee range during the third round, so just keep at it until it's nothing but a smoking hunk of rusted metal.

CAUTION

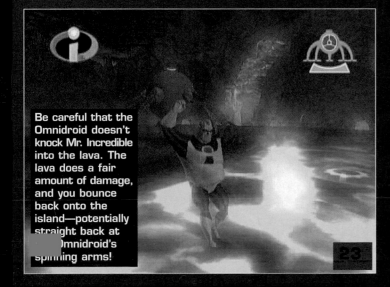

Be careful that the Omnidroid doesn't knock Mr. Incredible into the lava. The lava does a fair amount of damage, and you bounce back onto the island—potentially straight back at the Omnidroid's spinning arms!

BONUS ITEM

All three bonus items are hidden in the rocks. Keep an eye out for them!

ROBOT ARENA
CHAPTER 11

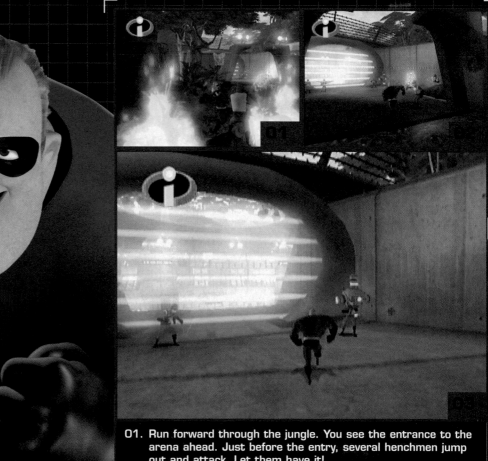

01. Run forward through the jungle. You see the entrance to the arena ahead. Just before the entry, several henchmen jump out and attack. Let them have it!
02. Enter the arena and be careful of the henchmen coming in from the two side rooms. Attack everyone in sight.
03. Run toward the generators and attack the laser gun henchmen guarding them. Grab the health power-up to the right after you've defeated the guards.

MR. INCREDIBLE

Enemies: Nomanisan Island Henchmen, Laser Gun Henchmen, Velocibots, Autoturrets, Tank

Mr. Incredible has returned to Nomanisan Island, and Syndrome's henchmen are here in full force. Mr. Incredible must find a means of entry into Syndrome's base, but it won't be easy—the place is guarded by some of the toughest foes yet!

CAUTION

The henchmen on this level group together, so they often attack simultaneously. Laser gun henchmen are more dangerous, as they have a ranged attack.

Both have a deadly close-range attack that is much more damaging than that of the henchmen you've fought previously. Use standard punches to save up your Incredi-Power for when you really need it!

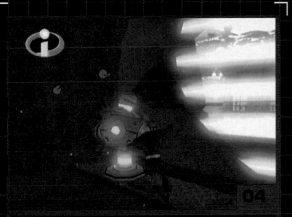

04. The henchmen continue pouring into the entryway. Wait for a break in the action then attack both the generators. This disables the security lasers barring entry to the arena proper.

NOTE

Two side passages lead from the main entrance to the arena, but both have security fields that can't be disabled from this side.

06. After you've disabled the lasers in the main entrance, a cutscene automatically has Mr. Incredible jump onto the velocipod.

07. You must destroy all three towers. Aim for the windows at the front of the towers to damage them.

08. Take a few moments to attack the velocibots and the henchmen firing from below—you won't be able to get all of them, but you should be able to eliminate some and decrease the damage you take.

TIP

When you pass behind a tower, shoot through the door. This does a great amount of damage.

BONUS ITEM

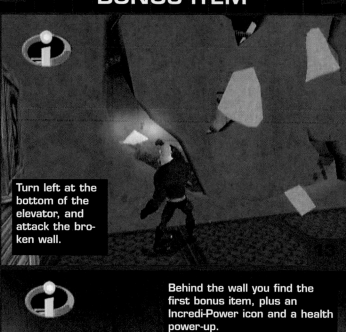

Turn left at the bottom of the elevator, and attack the broken wall.

Behind the wall you find the first bonus item, plus an Incredi-Power icon and a health power-up.

10. With the three towers destroyed, the velocipod crashes and Mr. Incredible is left vulnerable in the middle of the arena.
11. The remaining velocibots and henchmen continue attacking, so quickly turn left and head into the opening.
12. Take the elevator down to the underground level. Two laser gun henchmen guard the door to the right.

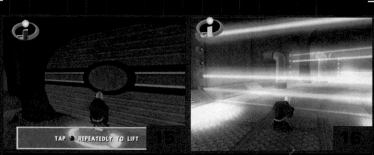

TAP ● REPEATEDLY TO LIFT

15. Stand on the marker near the door and lift. The door flies open. Activating the small consoles beside the door also opens it, so long as it isn't broken.
16. Run through the door. The hallway is blocked by security lasers. Crouch and roll under them.

TIP

Climb the large stack of crates in the center of the room to find an Incredi-Power icon.

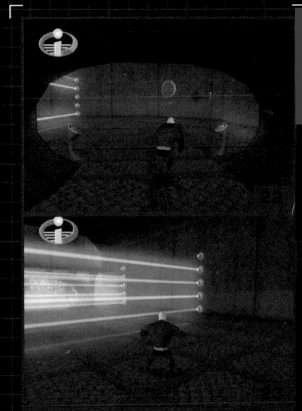

17. There are three security laser fields. Past the third one is a door. Stand on the marker near the door and force it open. Activating the small consoles beside the door also opens it, so long as it isn't broken.
18. The door opens, revealing a room filled with crates. Be careful as you move forward; several laser gun henchmen wait inside.
19. Two laser gun henchmen are standing on the opposite side of the first crates.
20. Three more laser gun henchmen guard the next door (one of these is hidden behind the crates). Either attack them with your fists or grab the nearby barrels and use them as projectiles.

22. Stand on the marker near the door and lift it. Run through the door and grab the health power-up.
23. Two laser fields block the next passage. Crouch and roll under them.

BONUS ITEM

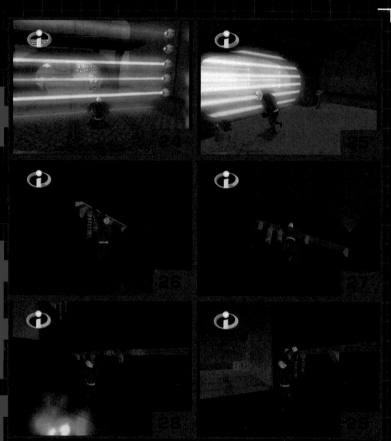

24. Be careful at the second laser field—laser gun henchmen fire at you from the control room ahead.

25. Roll under the lasers. Run into the control room and attack the henchmen. A security field activates at the doorway, preventing you from exiting the room.

26. Move through the control room into the small room on the opposite side. Turn left and jump up to grab the ledge.

27. Jump up and grab the second ledge. You can see an opening above, but you can't reach it from here. Jump to the left on to the small platform.

28. Run along the platform to the opposite wall. Jump up and grab the ledge, then shimmy to the left.

29. Jump to the next ledge, then jump into the opening to the left. Run down the hall to the intersection.

30. Turn left at the intersection and attack the broken wall.

31. Inside, you will find a bonus item and a health power-up.

32. Destroying the generators disables the nearby security lasers. The room beyond is one of the side chambers from the very beginning of the level!

33. Turn right at the intersection. You're on a walkway running along the inside of the arena. Attack the henchmen that appear—there are many of them, so use Incredi-Punches to make sure they stay down.
34. More henchmen emerge from the destroyed tower ahead. Eliminate them and keep moving forward.

NOTE

At the end of the walkway is a generator. Destroying this disables the lasers to the right. This is the second side area from the main entrance.

35. Run up the stairs at the end of the walkway, grabbing the health power-up on the way. The stairs lead to a small jungle area above.
36. Move forward and grab the Incredi-Power icon. Destroy the first autoturret, then move left and attack the second autoturret.

CAUTION

Be very cautious as you move through the area. The tower has a devastating attack. Steer clear of its beams—very clear. The beams are followed by a huge detonation that does a great deal of damage.

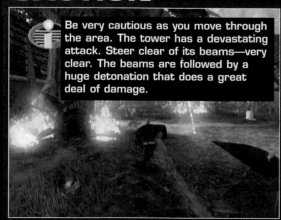

38. Run through the gate into the tank arena. As you enter, a laser field activates on the gate, trapping you inside. Grab the health power-up if you're hurt—the tank battle can be very tough.
39. The tank has four primary attacks. The first is two columns of laser fire. Jump over the lasers or duck beneath them to avoid them.
40. The second attack is a flamethrower. Jump over the flames. The tank makes two revolutions with the flamethrower, so you need to jump over the flames twice.
41. The third attack is a deadly beam. When you see it charging, quickly run around to the back of the tank.

BONUS ITEM

When you run around the tank, grab the bonus item from the upper-left corner of the arena.

After using its first three attacks, the tank fires bombs at Mr. Incredible. This is your chance to damage it! Pick up a bomb and lob it back.

CAUTION

The tank also has a fifth attack, which it deploys only when Mr. Incredible gets too close. This concussive wave knocks Mr. Incredible back, doing a great deal of damage in the process and preventing him from getting close enough to use his standard attack.

45. After you've hit the tank, it repeats its attacks in the same order. You need to hit it with three bombs to defeat it.
46. When the tank is destroyed, a new passage opens on the side of the arena. Run through to complete the level.

GREAT FALLS
CHAPTER 12

MR. INCREDIBLE

Enemy: OMNIDROID 09

It's time for a rematch! Mr. Incredible is attacked by the new-and-improved Omnidroid 09. It's faster, stronger, and it has some new attacks in its already-impressive arsenal. This isn't an easy battle, but Mr. Incredible has beaten this bot before.

01. Mr. Incredible's second bout with the Omnidroid is a bit tougher than the first. The Omnidroid is faster this time around, and can switch between attacks more rapidly. For the most part, though, you employ the same strategies as in the first battle.

02. The new Omnidroid has all of its older model's tricks, including its habit of ripping out huge chunks of ground and slamming them at Mr. Incredible.

03. As before, use the rocks as projectiles against the Omnidroid.

04. The ball is back as well, but this time it rolls faster. Remember to crouch and roll out of its way as it approaches. During the first round, the Omnidroid makes only one pass at Mr. Incredible while in ball form.

05. Run and dodge the Omnidroid's laser attack, and avoid the fiery trail it leaves behind. Recall that if you throw a rock at the turret when it's charging, the laser attack is aborted.

06. Attack the Omnidroid's legs with Incredi-Punches. Don't let up on the Omnidroid; attack constantly with punches and rocks.

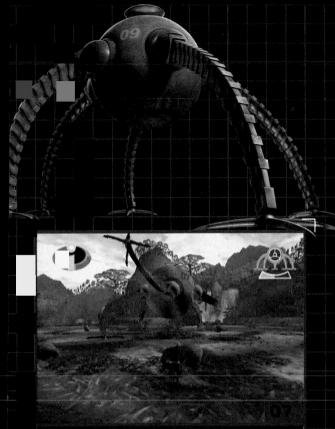

07. In addition to all of its old attacks, the Omnidroid has one new attack: whirling blades on the end of its appendages. It waves these blades wildly, but you can run around to its hind legs and attack while the blades are active.

TIP

Like the volcanic rocks, the rocks in Great Falls often contain Incredi-Power icons and health power-ups.

09. In addition to the whirling blades, the Omnidroid swipes and stabs at Mr. Incredible with its legs. Watch for this attack when moving in for melee attacks.
10. When the Omnidroid has taken a good deal of damage, it retreats across the water. It has something new up its sleeve, though. Or, rather, on its sleeve.
11. It releases one of its blades, sending it sailing at Mr. Incredible. Jump over the blade as it approaches. The blade makes three passes before returning to the Omnidroid, but if it connects it returns immediately.
12. After the blade attack, the Omnidroid begins hurling chunks of earth. Pick up the rocks and throw them at the Omnidroid. It jumps back to the island after its first defeat.

CAUTION

If Mr. Incredible is knocked into the water, get out as quickly as possible. Mines patrol the water and if they home in and attack, they do a great deal of damage.

TIP

Throw rocks at the Omnidroid while the blade makes its way back; it has no offensive attack during this brief period.

17. Keep attacking, using rocks and leg punches until the Omnidroid once again retreats across the water.
18. This time, the Omnidroid flings two blades at Mr. Incredible. Jump over them both as they approach. Stay alert and keep moving—they each make three passes, but have trouble hitting you if you keep moving.

13. During the second round, the Omnidroid's ball attack and top laser attack both happen twice. It makes two passes as the ball, and it attacks two times in sequence with the top laser.
14. The Omnidroid also deploys its bottom turret during the second round. Keep moving while this laser is firing to stay ahead of its blast.
15. As the bottom turret is firing, make your way toward the Omnidroid and, if you can get close enough, punch the turret.

TIP

It's more difficult to gather health during this battle because the Omnidroid fires its blades every time it changes position. But if you're hurt, it's worth the risk to break some rocks and find some health.

TIP

The flying Omnidroid blades can be attacked with a jumping Incredi-Attack if your timing is just right

20. When the Omnidroid begins tossing rocks, pick them up and throw them back. After its second defeat, it once again jumps to the island.
21. During this round, the Omnidroid's two primary attacks are tripled. It makes three attempts as the ball and fires its top laser three times.
22. The Omnidroid also employs its final attack—extending all of its appendages and spinning across the ground with its blades extended. This attack is more difficult to dodge in this second bout because the Omnidroid is faster. The blades also make it more damaging. Keep moving, jumping, and rolling to stay ahead of the deadly blades.
23. Continue attacking with rocks and punches. When the Omnidroid retreats for a third time, you're close to victory.

24. This time, it sends three blades at Mr. Incredible. Jump over all three blades, then keep moving and jumping to avoid them as they each make three more attempts to harm Mr. Incredible.
25. After the blades retreat, quickly pick up rocks and throw them at the Omnidroid. You want to take it out before you're forced to deal with the triple-blade threat a second time. When the Omnidroid is defeated, it makes one last futile leap at Mr. Incredible, then falls helplessly to the ground.

NOTE

After defeating the second Omnidroid, you can access Battle Mode from the pause menu. For Xbox, download Battle Mode using Xbox Live.

BONUS ITEMS

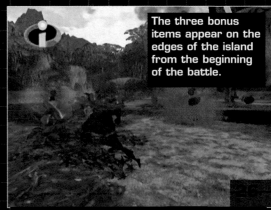

The three bonus items appear on the edges of the island from the beginning of the battle.

SYNDROME'S BASE
CHAPTER 13

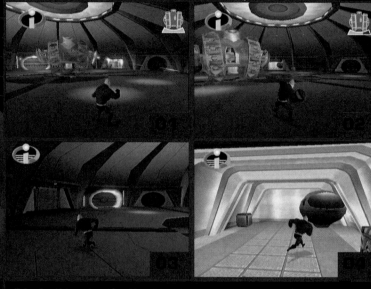

01. As if beating the Omnidroid a second time wasn't enough the first thing you face in Syndrome's base is a tank. Remember the strategy from Robot Arena and employ it here.
02. You have more room to maneuver than in the arena, which should make the battle easier. Hit the tank with three of its own bombs to destroy it.
03. The security lasers on the exit disappear when the tank is destroyed. But don't leave yet.
04. Two other small rooms are open. Run into the first, which is on the opposite side of the garage from the exit. A health power-up is hidden behind the car in the back.

BONUS ITEM

The second open door is to the right of the exit door. Inside, you find a health power-up and hidden behind the crates, the first bonus item.

MR. INCREDIBLE

Enemies: ARMORED HENCHMEN, FLYING LASER GUN HENCHMEN, TANK

Syndrome's Base is a fortress of maze-like corridors and tough security systems. And it's heavily guarded as well! Mr. Incredible must make his way past its many defenses and one of the toughest of all is waiting for him right at the entrance.

TIP

When fighting armored henchmen, use standard punches against small numbers. But always use Incredi-Punches when dealing with large groups.

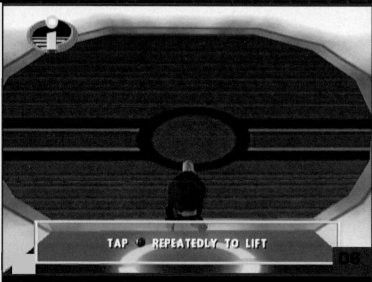

TAP ● REPEATEDLY TO LIFT

06

06. Go to the exit and stand on the marker. Lift the door to force it open.

07. Run up the sloped hallway. Dodge the fire from the ceiling-mounted turret, then jump and punch it when in range.
08. Use the console to open the door.
09. When you enter the hub room, you see that rotating lasers protect the floor.
10. Run down the steps to the floor and turn right. Run toward the next platform, jumping over the beams as they approach from behind.

11. On the second platform, you encounter two armored henchmen. These are tougher than standard henchmen, and can take a great deal more damage before going down for the count.
12. You can find a health power-up in some crates on the platform's lower level.
13. Use the console on the control panel to shut off the lasers on the exit door.

TIP

Before leaving the hub room, search the floor for a health power-up. There's more fighting ahead, and you've most likely taken some damage.

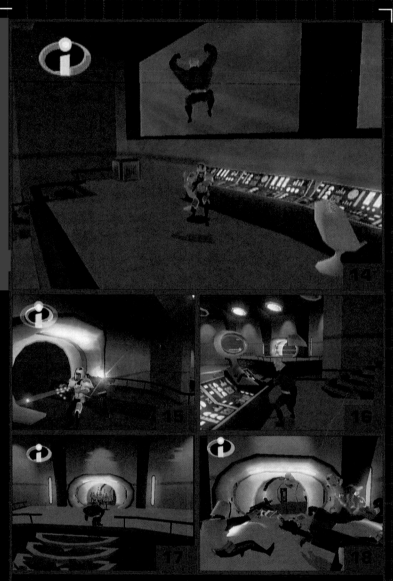

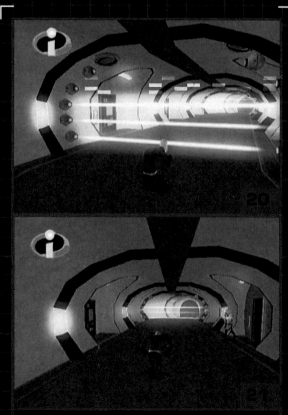

14. Go down the stairs and turn right. Run to the next platform. Jump on to the higher level and attack the armored henchman.
15. Turn around and run toward the upper platform. Jump up to the platform and attack the henchman.
16. Jump back down and run over to the console. Use the console to disable the floor lasers. Run down to the floor.
17. Climb the steps to the door, which is now accessible. A large group of armored henchmen runs in through the door. Use a jumping Incredi-Punch to do damage to all of them.
18. The jumping attack knocks them down, but most get back up. Keep swinging until they're all defeated.

20. Run through the now open door into the hallway. It's protected by security lasers. Crouch and roll under the first set of lasers.
21. An armored henchman emerges from a door to the right. Attack him. Inside the room you will find a health power-up.

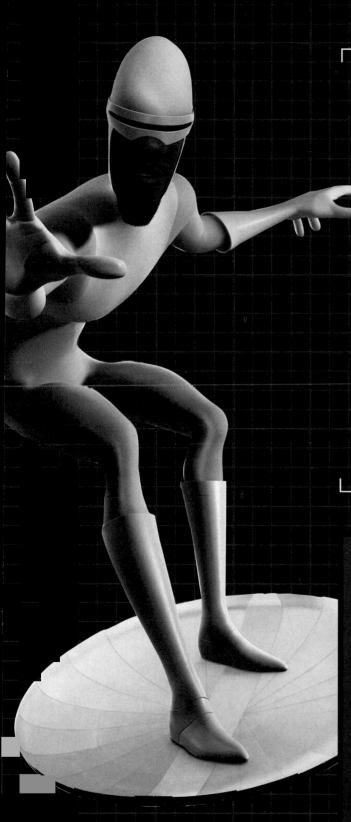

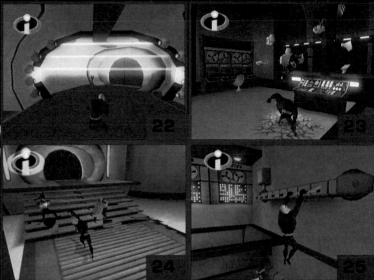

22. Crouch and roll under the second set of security lasers. Use the console to open the door.
23. Run past the computers and attack the henchman standing at the console.
24. Another henchman enters from the elevator. Attack him as well.
25. Go back to the entrance. Facing the door, you will see two bars on the wall to the left. Jump up and climb these bars to the elevated walkway.

TIP

If you're injured, destroy the crate on the walkway to find a health power-up.

27. Move to the end of the walkway and turn left. Jump onto the computer.
28. Jump from the computer to the lamp and then swing and jump to the second computer. Jump from the computer to the second walkway.
29. Turn right. Run toward the henchman, grab him, and throw him off the walkway. You can find a health power-up behind the crates nearby.

30. Turn around and run down the walkway to the device. Grab it and rotate it. The elevator doors open.
31. Jump down from the walkway and enter the elevator. Grab the Incredi-Power icon inside.
32. Exit the elevator, turn left, and run down the stairs. Attack the two henchmen standing at the controls. One of these henchmen is on the other side of the raised area.
33. Drop down to the lower level and immediately run to the console. Use it to open the laser-blocked door above. The console also disables the wall turrets and activates the lift nearby.
34. Attack the henchmen on this level, and then ride the lift to the upper area.
35. Grab the device and turn it. This rotates the central platform in the hub room as well as extends the bridges to the platform.
36. You don't have much time to make it to the hub room. A large group of henchmen attacks. Use a jumping Incredi-Punch to knock them down, but don't stick around to finish them off.
37. Go through the doors into the hallway. It's blocked by three sets of lasers. Crouch and roll under them.

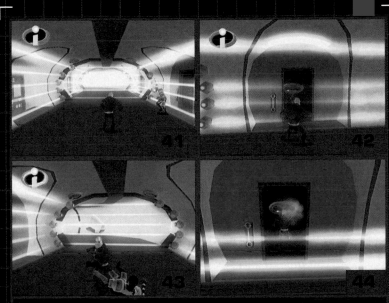

41. The hall is, once again, filled with lasers. But these not only block movement forward, but to the sides as well.
42. Move forward. A henchman appears from a side room. Attack him, then turn and face the room. The lasers disappear for brief intervals. When they're down, run into the room and use the console.
43. Wait for the lasers to shut off again and then run out of the room. You can now move forward to the next section of the hall. Another henchman emerges from a side room. Attack him.
44. Once again, wait for the laser to shut off and then run into the room. Use the console. Quickly leave the room when the side lasers flicker off.

BONUS ITEM

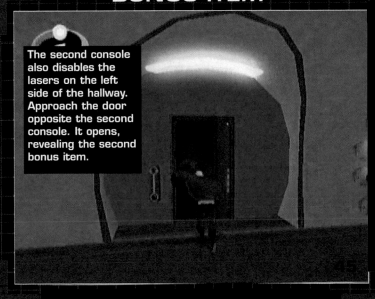

The second console also disables the lasers on the left side of the hallway. Approach the door opposite the second console. It opens, revealing the second bonus item.

38. Two henchmen emerge from a small side room before you reach the third set of lasers. Quickly attack them. You can find an Incredi-Power icon through the door to the left, but it's best to keep moving.
39. Roll under the third laser field and run out the door. Keep moving across the bridge to the platform, where you find a health power-up.
40. Continue across the second bridge and use the console to open the door. Go into the hall.

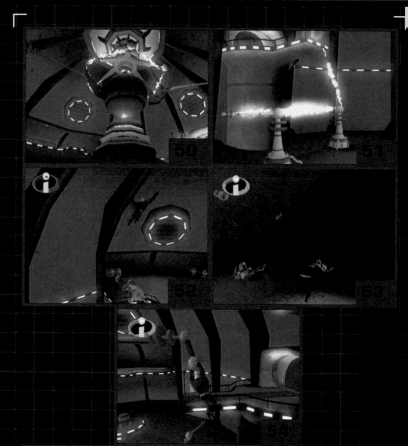

46. Crouch and roll under the last laser barrier, then run to the end of the hall and use the console to open the door.
47. The door leads to the generator room. Your first goal is to eliminate the henchmen on the ground floor.

TIP

Instead of fighting the henchmen *mano a mano*, there is a quicker way: Just pick them up and toss them into the gap in the floor.

50. Jump across the gap to the center device. Grab it and rotate. This temporarily shuts off the electricity above, and causes the machine to rotate.
51. Go to the third device, and grab and rotate it. This temporarily shuts off the electricity surging through the posts nearby.
52. Now you must act very quickly. Run over to the nearest post, jump up, and grab it. Release the post, and Mr. Incredible flies up to a platform on the upper level.
53. Henchmen occupy the platform, but there's no time to fight. Use a jumping Incredi-Punch to stun them. Don't waste time fighting them—the generator stops rotating soon, and if it does you have to drop down and turn all the devices again.
54. Jump to one of the generator's arms, which are quickly moving by. Hang onto the arm until you reach the next platform, then drop off, grab the Incredi-Power icon and go through the doors.

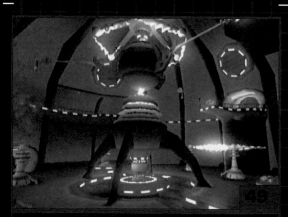

49. Stand near the entry door and face the generator. Run to the device to the right, grab it, and rotate it. This momentarily shuts off the electricity around the center device.

NOTE

If you want to eliminate all the enemies in the room, you need to launch Mr. Incredible with the second set of posts on the opposite side of the room from the third device. This launches him to a different platform on the upper level, where more henchmen await.

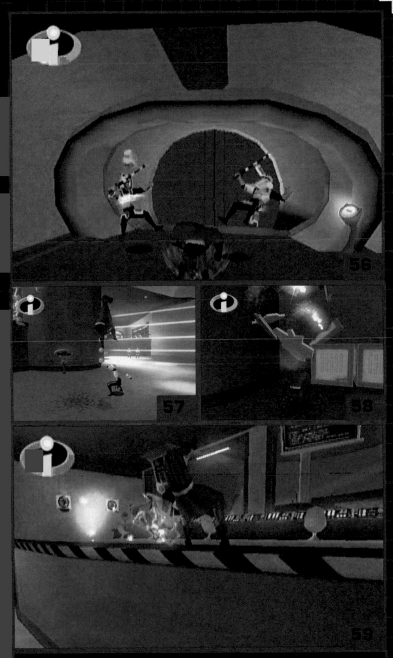

TIP

If you climb up the wall next to the turrets, they won't be able to hit you when you reach the second tier.

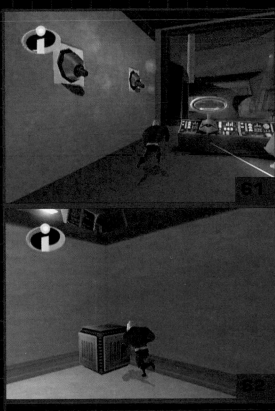

56. Two more henchmen guard the console at the end of the short hall. Attack them and then use the console to open the door.
57. Run down the steps and immediately attack the henchman near security lasers on the ground floor. Use the console, which activates the lift in the room beyond the lasers.
58. A health power-up is behind the crates on the ground floor, to the right of the lasers.
59. More henchmen jump down from the upper level. Attack them. Jump and climb the wall to the second tier of the room. Run over and attack the wall turrets to destroy them.

61. Use the console near the turrets. This disables the security laser on the ground floor. Drop back down and attack the henchmen guarding the lift.
62. If you're low on health, break the crate near the lift for a health power-up.

PRESS ⊕ TO ACTIVATE CONSOLE

63. Ride the lift to the second tier and eliminate all the henchmen guarding the area.
64. When the coast is clear, use the console near the lasers. It deactivates two nearby laser fields, including one protecting a console.
65. Run to the console and use it. This activates another console next to the door leading out of this area.

66. Run to the door, use the console, and head into the hall.
67. Fight the henchmen who approach. There is a console halfway down the hallway; use it to open the door at the far end.
68. Mr. Incredible emerges in the top level of the hub room. The bridges to the center area retract and two doors on either side of the room open, sending a horde of henchmen running his way.
69. Fight the henchmen if you're feeling feisty, but your main task is to activate the two consoles near the railing. The henchmen keep coming, so don't try to fight them all.
70. When the consoles are activated, the first bridge extends. Run to the center area.

71. Two more henchmen drop down and attack. Take them out and then activate the console to the left. Grab the Incredi-Power icon near the console.

72. Run across the second bridge. You see a device directly ahead. When you reach the other side, more henchmen will emerge from two side rooms.

PRESS ⬤ TO RELEASE DEVICE

BONUS ITEM

Turn left and run up the steps after the second bridge.

Enter the left-hand side room. The third bonus item is hidden behind the crates in the upper-right corner. You will also find a health power-up nearby.

75. In addition to armored henchmen, flying laser gun henchmen attack after the second bridge. Grab an armored henchman and use him as a projectile against his airborne associates.

76. Grab the device and turn it. This lowers an elevator in the center area.

77. Return to the center area via the bridge and jump on the elevator.

78. After the elevator reaches its destination, run down the hallway and through the mysterious door at the end.

FINDING MR. INCREDIBLE

CHAPTER 14

01. Move forward to the chasm. There's a branch hanging above. Swing from the branch to the opposite side.
02. Mrs. Incredible automatically hitches a ride into the base.
03. Move down the hallway. A henchman jumps out of a door to the right. Attack him. More henchmen come around the corner ahead. Grab them and toss them around until the hall is clear.

TIP

Grab the Incredi-Power icon from the now open door on the right!

MRS. INCREDIBLE

Enemies: NOMANISAN ISLAND HENCHMEN, LASER GUN HENCHMEN, LOBBER HENCHMEN

Mrs. Incredible has ventured to Nomanisan Island to find out what her husband is up to. She must sneak into Syndrome's base and fight her way through an army of minions.

04. The hallway ends at a closed elevator and an intersection. Lasers block the passage to the left. Turn right. Use the console to open the door.
05. Run into the control room and activate the console. Grab the health power-up inside if Mrs. Incredible has taken damage. Otherwise, save it for a moment.

PRESS ⊡ TO ACTIVATE CONSOLE

06. Activating the console lowers the lasers in the hallway. It also summons a large group of henchmen. Fight them all before proceeding.

BONUS ITEM

In addition to lowering the lasers, the first console also opens the elevator in the hallway. Go inside to find the first bonus item.

08. Go down the newly accessible hallway. Wall turrets open fire from the left wall; destroy them with standard attacks. Activate the console to open the door.

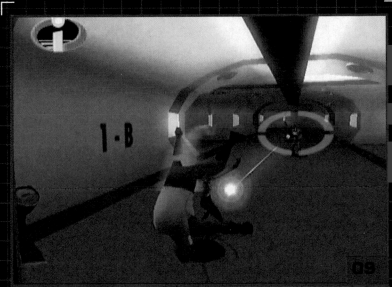

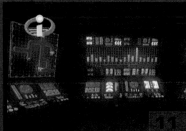

09. Two laser gun henchmen are guarding the hallway. Attack them, then run forward.
10. As you approach the intersection, laser fields appear on two passages, leaving only the left-hand passage accessible. Henchmen approach from the left.
11. Attack the henchmen, go left into corridor 1-C, and use the console to open the door. Activate the console inside the control room.
12. The console removes one of the laser fields in the hallway, and summons a large group of henchmen. Fight them and then return to the intersection.
13. Turn left at the intersection into the corridor with the search lights. Two laser gun henchmen guard the hall. Attack them, then continue down the corridor. More henchmen attack.

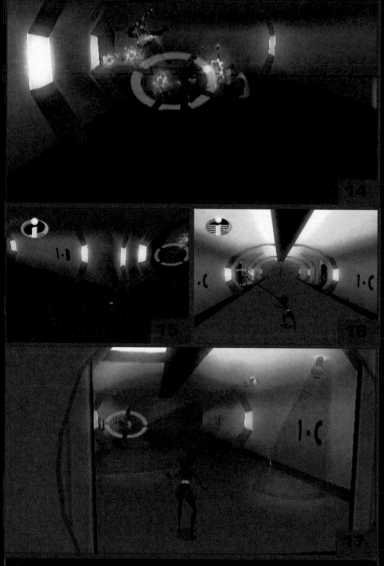

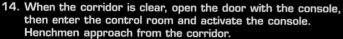

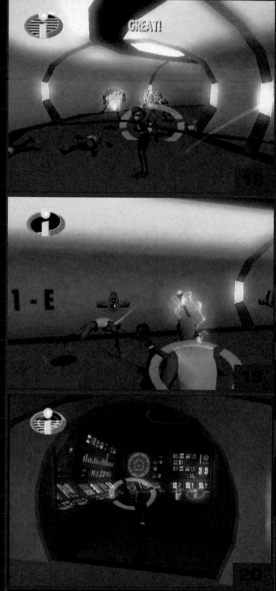

14. When the corridor is clear, open the door with the console, then enter the control room and activate the console. Henchmen approach from the corridor.

15. As you return to the intersection, laser gun henchmen emerge from side doors. Fight them, then grab an Incredi-Power icon from the room to the right and a health power-up from the room to the left.

16. Turn left at the intersection. Henchmen emerge from the doors on either side of the hallway. After they're defeated, look in the side rooms for a health power-up and an Incredi-Power icon.

17. Proceed down the hall to the door and use the console to open it. You won't be able to access the door ahead (or the visible bonus item), so turn left into corridor 1-D.

18. A large group of henchmen attacks at the bend. Use Mrs. Incredible's Incredi-Punch to take them all out quickly.

19. Run toward corridor 1-E, destroying the wall turrets on the way. More henchmen are waiting at the intersection. Fight them, then grab the health power-up from the room across from the turrets. T right into corridor 1-E.

20. Use the console to open the door. A_ the two henchmen in the console roor and grab the Incredi-Power icon inside

BONUS ITEM

The door to the bonus item has opened, and you can run into the corridor to grab it.

24. The console activates the machine in the center of the room. Grab onto its arm as it passes by and ride it to the platform.

TIP

If Mrs. Incredible needs an extra health power-up at any point during the next sequence, you can find one on the floor of this room.

22. Activate the console in the control room. This disables the lasers in corridor 1-E. Several henchmen emerge from the room down the hall. Three of the henchmen use shields to prevent Mrs. Incredible from attacking. Grab the non-shielded henchmen and throw them at their protected cohorts.

23. Run straight down the hall to the room at the opposite end. Use the console near the door.

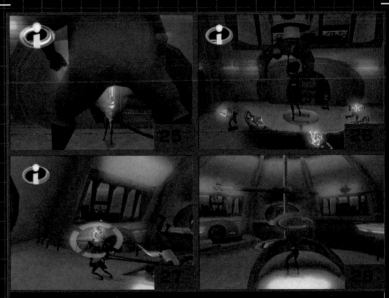

25. Drop to the platform when the arm extends. Attack the henchmen. Grab the health power-up. Activate the console when the platform is cleared.

26. Grab the arm as it passes by, then ride it to the next platform. Drop down and attack the henchmen. Grab the health power-up when the battle is over and activate the console on this platform.

27. Grab the machine's arm. It rises and carries Mrs. Incredible to the first upper platform. Drop down and attack. Activate this console, then ride the machine's arm to the next platform.

28. More henchmen are waiting. Fight them, then activate this platform's console. Ride the arm to the next platform. The nearby door leads out of this room.

BONUS ITEM

Before leaving the room, activate the last console, then ride the arm to the fourth upper platform. Fight the henchmen, then run into the rear room to find the third bonus item. Ride the arm back to the platform with the exit door.

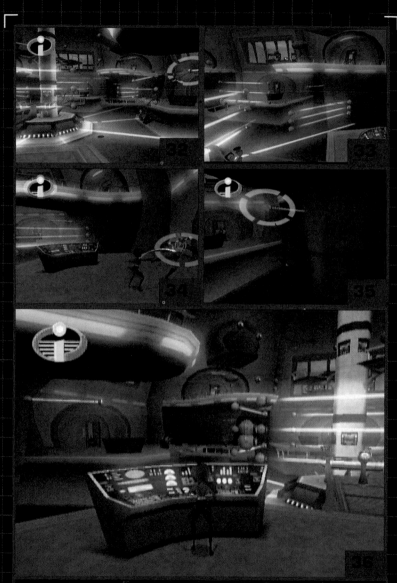

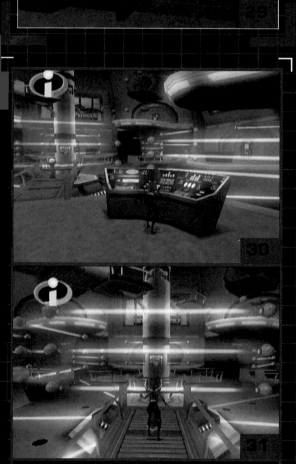

30. Run down the corridor into the next room. Inside, you find a complex series of platforms protected by security lasers. Activate both consoles on the platform.

31. This disables the security lasers on the short bridge ahead. Run forward and activate the console on the bridge. The security lasers to the right of the platform are disabled.

32. Leave the bridge and move to the edge of the platform and stand near the now-exposed pole. Target the pole and then swing to the next platform.

33. On the next platform, once again use both consoles and then run out on the bridge to the newly exposed console. This exposes a second pole. Swing from it to the next platform.

34. A group of henchmen emerges from the door on this platform. Fight them and then grab the health power-up from the small room from which they appeared.

35. Then use the two nearby consoles, followed by the console on the bridge. Swing from the third pole to the next platform.

36. Henchmen also guard the fourth platform. Attack them, then grab the health power-up inside the room at the back of the platform. Use the two consoles once the henchmen are gone.

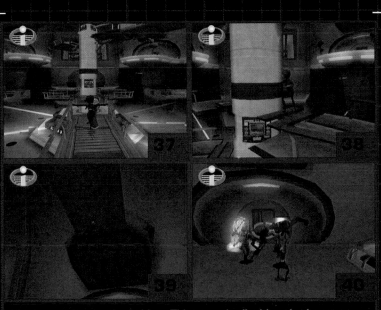

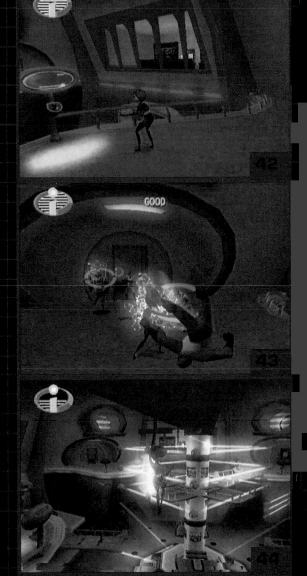

37. Run out onto the bridge. This console disables the lasers blocking the controls in the center of the room.
38. Jump from the bridge to the center platforms. Use the controls. The platform rises, carrying Mrs. Incredible to the second level.
39. Wait for the rotating bridge overhead to pass by. Grab the small handle on the underside of the bridge, then let go when Mrs. Incredible is dangling over the platform.
40. Fight the henchmen guarding the platform. Run into the adjacent room for an Incredi-Power icon, then return to the platform.

41. Use both consoles on this platform. When both have been activated, grab onto the bridge as it passes overhead and hang on until you reach the next platform.

42. On the second upper platform, use both of the consoles. Then once again grab onto the bridge, and let it carry you to the third platform.
43. Another henchmen ambush awaits. Defeat them all, grab the Incredi-Power icon from the adjacent room, then use both the consoles.
44. Grab the bridge and move to the fourth upper platform. More henchmen attack. Fight them and grab the health power-up from the nearby room.

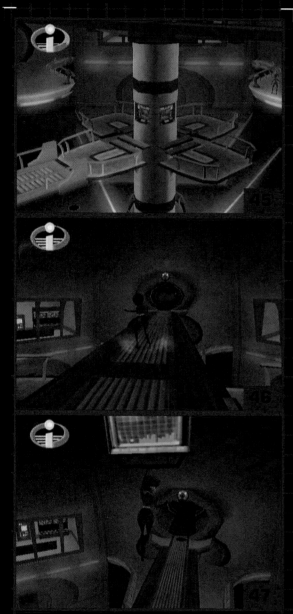

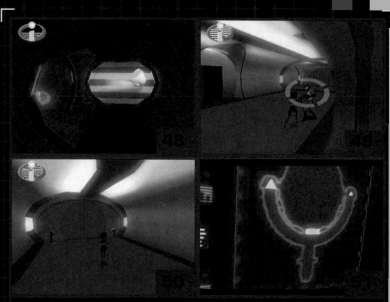

48. After the turret fires, drop down onto the bridge and run into the tunnel. Turn left at the lasers and grab the Incredi-Power icon.
49. Enter the corridor and turn right. Attack the two henchmen and continue moving down the hall.
50. At the intersection, turn right. Attack the henchmen in the corridor, then proceed to the end. Use the console to open the door and then enter the control room. Activate the console.
51. When the console is activated, you will see a change in the diagram on the wall—one of the yellow triangles vanishes.

45. Use both consoles on the final platform. This lowers the lasers around the central column. Ride the bridge around the room to the platform with the bridge.
46. Henchmen attack when Mrs. Incredible lands on the platform. Fight them, then run across the bridge to the center column. Activate the console on the column and the platform rises to the bridge.
47. Jump onto the bridge. A wall-mounted turret near the exit begins firing. Grab onto the box hanging over the bridge to dodge its fire.

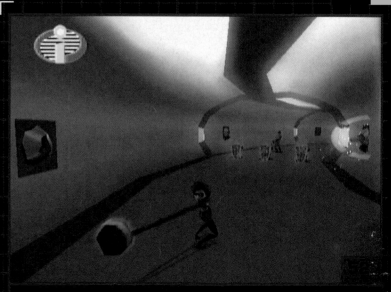

52. Turn around and return to the corridor. It is now heavily guarded. Lobber henchmen and several shielded henchmen are positioned outside the door. Additionally, wall turrets have appeared throughout the corridor. Grab the bombs and toss them at the henchmen and turrets.

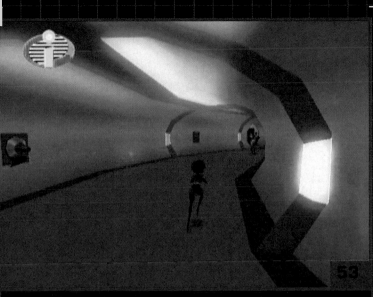

53. Grab the health power-up from the control room, then continue down the hall. Turrets have appeared throughout, so use standard attacks to destroy them as you move.

58. Run down the hallway to the center door. More henchmen are waiting at the intersection. Attack if you want, or just turn left at the intersection to go through the door and complete the mission.

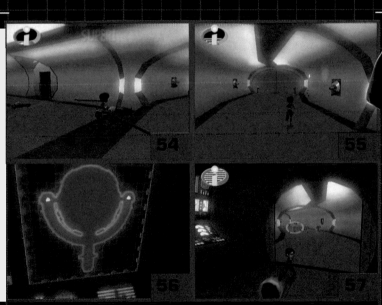

54. At the intersection, more henchmen—including lobber henchmen—attack. Use the bombs on the turrets and then use melee attacks on the henchmen themselves.

55. Keep moving down the hall, attacking the turrets and any remaining henchmen. Use the console at the end of the hall to open the door.

56. Enter the control room and activate the console. The diagram shows that the center door is open. Grab the health power-up and Incredi-Power icon from the control room.

57. A group of henchmen appears outside the control room. Once again, use the lobber henchmen's bombs to take out the shielded henchmen, then attack them.

100-MILE DASH
CHAPTER 15

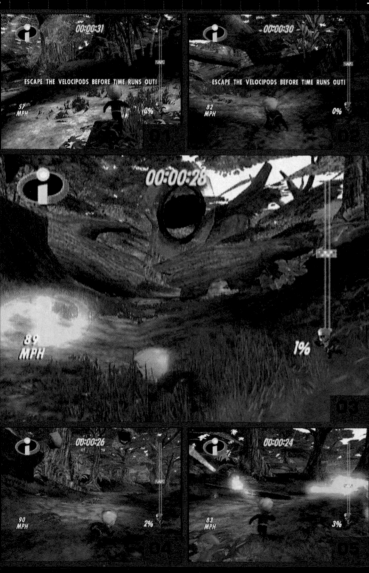

01. In this Dash level, you have a predetermined amount of time to make it from one checkpoint to the next.
02. Turn left at the first bend and run under the fallen tree.
03. Grab the Incredi-Power icon in the path and then run through the gap in the tree trunk ahead.
04. Use Incredi-Boost after the tree trunk and follow the path as it bends to the right.
05. Jump over the log in the road. Follow the path down into the cave.

DASH

Enemies: VELOCIPODS
Dash must race through the jungle to avoid the pursuing velocipods! Unlike the previous Dash level, there isn't an overall time limit. Instead, you have short time limits between each checkpoint. Remember to use Incredi-Boosts whenever the opportunity presents itself so the velocipods won't catch Dash!

BONUS ITEM

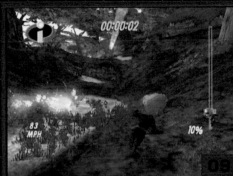

As you approach the second cave, veer to the right and take the small path that leads over it.

The first bonus item is on top of the cave, just before the first checkpoint.

06. Move to the left side of the tunnel to avoid the rock, then immediately move to the right side of the cave. Run past the second rock and out of the cave.
07. The path bends to the right. Jump over the log in the road. Another log is just ahead. Jump over it as well.
08. The road bends to the right again. Jump over the log at the bend.

11. If you enter the second cave, grab the Incredi-Power icon in the path.
12. Jump over the log past the cave. The first checkpoint is just ahead.
13. Dash runs under a fallen tree. Immediately jump over the first log. Follow the path right and jump over the next log, another cave is just ahead.
14. Dash's incredible speed allows him to defy gravity and run up the walls of caves. Use this technique to avoid the boulders.

15. There are four boulders in the cave. The first is on the right, the second on the left, the third is directly in the center, and the final boulder is on the left.
16. Use Incredi-Boost as you exit the cave to reach the second checkpoint.
17. Jump over the log just past the second checkpoint. Another log is ahead. Run around it or jump over it. You see water on the horizon.

18. Dash is moving so quickly he can skim across the water's surface! You can use Incredi-Boost while running on water with no friction damage. Stay to the right to avoid the falling rocks.
19. When Dash reaches the beach, veer right to find the next path.
20. The path ahead is clear, so use Incredi-Boost to speed up. Make sure you keep to the right to stay on the path.
21. At the 29 percent mark, you see a sloping ramp ahead. Use Incredi-Boost to speed up the ramp.
22. Jump from the top of the ramp to clear the chasm, then immediately pull to the right to stay on the path. The third checkpoint is right after the chasm.
23. Run onto the bridge and grab the Incredi-Power icon.
24. After the bridge, the path veers left. Stay with the path, but note the small outcropping to the right. This is important in a moment.
25. Jump over the log, then follow the path as it continues turning to the left.

BONUS ITEM

The second bonus item is right on the path at the 42 percent mark.

26. Grab the Incredi-Power icon in the path, then leap over the log as the path straightens out.
27. The path turns left again. There's a bridge ahead. This is actually the same bridge—you've just made a loop. Remember the outcropping? It's about to become important.
28. As Dash crosses the bridge a second time, a velocipod destroys the boulders on the outcropping, revealing a new path. Jump the small gap onto the outcropping.
29. Follow the new path as it bends to the left. It's a fairly clear road, so use an Incredi-Boost.

31. You drop from a small cliff after the second bonus item. Begin veering right when you see the next bridge ahead.
32. Cross the bridge. The path turns sharply right under a log, then turns left immediately.

33. The path leads up, bending sharply to the left. When the path levels and straightens out, use an Incredi-Boost to speed through the next flat area.

34. You see a waterfall ahead, and what appears to be a dead end.

35. Run past the waterfall. Dash automatically jumps at the end of the path and swings to the next section.

36. After Dash lands, use an Incredi-Boost to reach the next checkpoint.

37. The path returns to the deep jungle. Follow it as it veers left, and jump over the first log.

38. Things get crazy up ahead, with several logs and some significant velocipod fire. Stay on the path and jump any logs that aren't destroyed.

39. At the 58 percent mark, you enter another cave. Stay left to avoid the first boulder.

40. Keep left to avoid the second boulder, then veer right to avoid the third.

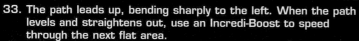

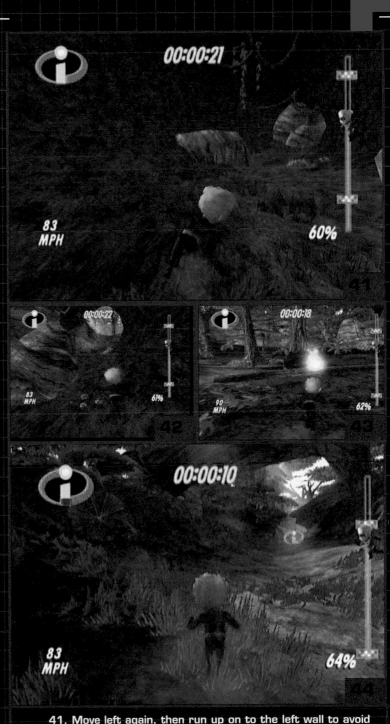

41. Move left again, then run up on to the left wall to avoid the last two boulders, both of which are situated on the left side.
42. Make a complete loop, running across the roof of the cave and down to the floor just before the exit.
43. More logs lie in the path ahead. Jump over all four.
44. Grab the Incredi-Power icon and stay in the center of the

45. Jump over the next two logs in the road. The checkpoint is after the second log. Jump over the next two logs immediately after the checkpoint.
46. Run under the rock arch. You see another lake on the horizon.
47. Run across the lake, avoiding the large rocks that tumble down as the velocipods fire at them.

48. The next section of the path is clear. Use Incredi-Boost to gain some ground.
49. Dash falls off a small cliff to the jungle floor below. The checkpoint is just after the cliff.
50. After the checkpoint, move to the center of the path to run through the tree trunk.
51. There's a cave just after the trunk. Stay left to avoid the first boulder and keep left to avoid the second.
52. Run up the left wall of the cave to avoid the third and fourth boulders, located at the right and left of the cave, respectively.
53. Jump over the log sitting in the path just after the cave exit.
54. Veer right up on to the slope to grab the Incredi-Power icon and avoid the log.
55. Another log blocks the path. Jump over it and enter the small cave. Grab the Incredi-Power icon.

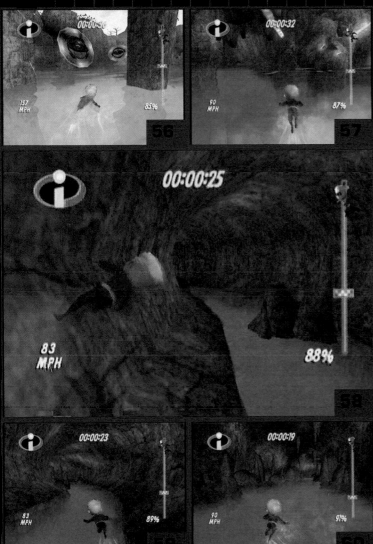

61. Follow the water as it twists through the large rocks. It bends to the left.

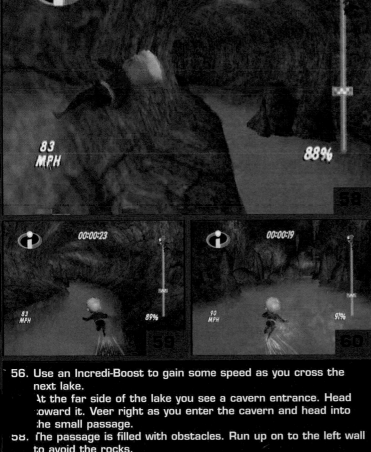

BONUS ITEM

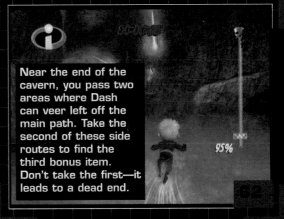

Near the end of the cavern, you pass two areas where Dash can veer left off the main path. Take the second of these side routes to find the third bonus item. Don't take the first—it leads to a dead end.

63. At around the 95 percent mark, you see the cavern exit. Run through the exit to complete the race.

56. Use an Incredi-Boost to gain some speed as you cross the next lake.

   At the far side of the lake you see a cavern entrance. Head toward it. Veer right as you enter the cavern and head into the small passage.

58. The passage is filled with obstacles. Run up on to the left wall to avoid the rocks.

59. Run up and across the roof to avoid the second set of rocks, then stay right to avoid the third set of rocks as you return to the floor.

60. Run up the right wall to avoid the next two rocks and then stay to the left after you reach the floor. You emerge in a large passage.

VIOLET'S CROSSING

CHAPTER 16

! CAUTION

Walking into plants alerts henchmen and they will fire at Violet even while invisible.

VIOLET

Enemies: LASER GUN HENCHMEN
She is the only member of the family with two known powers and a great way to avoid fighting: She can turn herself invisible and also defend herself with a force field! In this level, use Violet's invisibility power to sneak through the jungle past Syndrome's guards.

01. You begin near a rock and an Incredi-Power icon. Stand on the marker near the rock and watch the henchman's patrol pattern.
02. Become invisible and run by the first henchman.

PRESS ⬤ TO RESUME **03**

PRESS ⬤ TO RESUME **04**

05

07

CAUTION

Don't get too close to the henchmen! If Violet brushes against them, she alerts them to her presence.

BONUS ITEM

Move forward slightly and watch the henchmen ahead. When he turns his back, run forward and grab the bonus item. Go invisible as you run back to the slope.

08

PRESS ⬤ TO RESUME **09**

03. Run to the next rock. Watch the henchman on the cliff above. When his back is turned, run over and grab the Incredi-Power icon.

04. Turn around and follow the path a short way to the next rock. Again, watch the henchman's pattern. Wait for him to turn his back and begin walking back to the beginning of his route.

05. Run out from behind the rock and move up behind the henchman. Become invisible and run up the slope to the left.

06. At the top of the slope, grab the Incredi-Power icon.

08. Wait on the slope for the henchman below to pass by. Use invisibility and run forward through the gate.

09. Stand on the marker and watch the henchmen. One begins moving toward Violet's position.

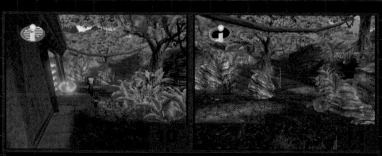

10. When he begins moving away, run up behind him. Use invisibility as he turns around. Grab the Incredi-Power icon.
11. Run to the right and up the slope.

TIP

You can also dodge these henchmen by running around the building. Go invisible as you turn the corner, and then make a dash for the slope.

13. At the top of the slope, grab the Incredi-Power icon and stand on the marker. Watch the henchmen below.
14. When the henchmen on the left moves out of view, jump off the slope, use invisibility, and run forward. Grab the Incredi-Power icon, and stay invisible.
15. Run past the henchman guarding the center of the area, then make for the gate, dodging the next henchman.
16. Stand on the marker next to the building and watch the henchmen patrol pattern.

BONUS ITEM

The second bonus item is behind the building just past the second gate.

18. Run to the rock ahead and left. Grab the Incredi-Power icon. Wait for the first henchman to pass, then use invisibility and run forward.
19. Pass the second henchman and run around the rocks to the marker.

BONUS ITEM

Run around the henchman near the gate and turn right. You see a cave ahead. Take cover behind the rocks and wait a moment for Violet's Incredi-Power to recharge.

Use invisibility and run for the cave. Inside, you find the third bonus item.

Wait for Violet's Incredi-Power to recharge, then exit the cave and run past the final henchman and out the gate.

20. Stand on the marker and watch the patrol. Wait until both henchmen begin moving left, then run out from behind the rock.
21. Stay on the right-hand path, and go invisible as you pass the second rock.
22. Pass the second henchman and bolt around the rocks to the marker. Grab the Incredi-Power icon, and then stand on the marker and look.
23. When the nearest henchman begins walking away, run out and use invisibility. Stay to the right, between the wall and the rocks.
24. Dart left through the gap in the rocks and grab the Incredi-Power icon. Remain invisible and run forward.
25. Veer right and grab the next Incredi-Power icon. Keep Invisibility active.
26. Run forward toward the gate. This is the exit, but there's one more bonus item to find.

INCREDI-BALL
CHAPTER 17

01. Roll forward along the path. Take this opportunity to familiarize yourself with the controls. You can slow the Incredi-Ball by pulling back and speed it up by pressing forward. Move left and right to turn.
02. Speed along the path and crash through the tree trunks at the end. The Incredi-Ball can destroy some objects it hits, which is important as you proceed.
03. Roll forward toward the gate ahead. Note the ramp-like structure and the laser generator above the gate. Two henchmen guard the gate—smash into them to eliminate them.
04. Roll up the ramp and destroy the laser generator. This opens the gate below.

DASH AND VIOLET

Enemies: NOMANISAN ISLAND HENCHMEN, LASER GUN HENCHMEN, VELOCIPODS, AUTOTURRETS
Dash and Violet use their powers in tandem to create the powerful Incredi-Ball! Guide the Incredi-Ball through the maze-like compound to meet up with Mr. and Mrs. Incredible.

TIP

Before going through the gate, turn around and find the cave to the right of the ramp on the opposite side of the area.

Roll through the cave and destroy the generator at the end of this small path. This is the first of three optional generators on this level. Destroying all three gives you access to the final bonus item.

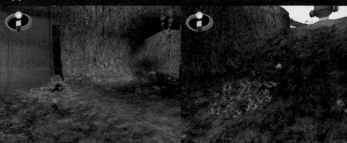

07. Roll through the now-open gate. Roll into any henchmen in your path, and continue down to the next open area.
08. The next area is heavily fortified. Autoturrets, a Viper, and a small army of henchmen are waiting. Roll into anything and everything.

TIP

Several health power-ups can be found along the walls of the area. Look for them if the Incredi-Ball has taken too much damage.

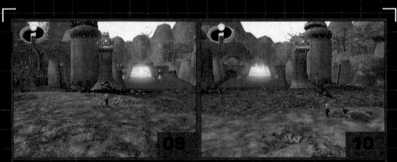

09. Get some momentum and roll toward the ramp-like pillar next to the first gate. Roll up the pillar and smash the generator.
10. Make another pass through the area to get momentum, then roll up the second pillar and destroy the generator. This opens the gate.

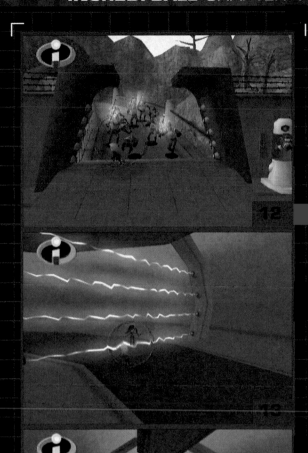

12. Roll through the gate. Henchmen stand in the entrance like bowling pins. Knock them over as you pass through.
13. Roll up the ramp and into the tunnel. Four walls of electricity block the path. Watch the pattern, and roll through when the electricity is off.
14. Two autoturrets guard the exit of the tunnel. Roll through the last field when it shuts off and then continue right past the turrets.

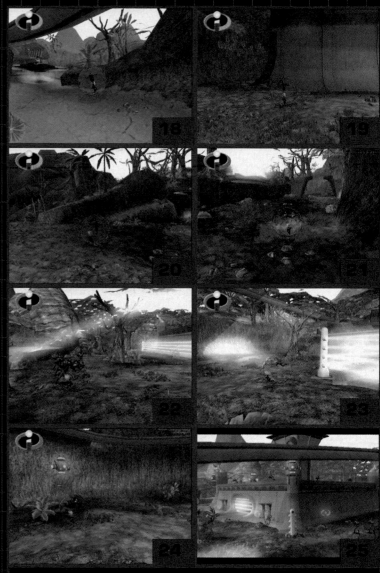

15. Exit the tunnel on to the small road. The road ends just before the waterfall.
16. Roll up on to the wall to the right to make it over the gap and into the tunnel behind the waterfall.
17. Stay on the path to the left of the next gate and watch for the autoturrets that attack as you approach.

18. Stay on the path as it passes under the track. Smash into the velocipod at the end of the path.
19. You land in the first area. If you're hurt, health power-ups are scattered about, including two on the large ramp under the track.
20. Opposite this ramp, you will see a velocipod at the end of a small sloping path. Roll up the path and smash into the velocipod. It crashes into the generator, opening the next area.
21. Roll through the next gate. Speed along the path to the next area, a heavily fortified building with a tower.
22. The area has several dangers. Four lasers guard the building and numerous henchman chase you.
23. Additionally, a powerful beam attacks the Incredi-Ball if it hits any of the spotlights searching the area. Do your best to avoid them.
24. You need to disable the lasers on the building. There are four generators on the walls surrounding the area. Roll up the walls and smash all four generators; each removes a laser.
25. When the fourth laser is disabled, the building is no longer surrounded, but the interior is still inaccessible. You can, however, grab some of the health power-ups around its border if needed.

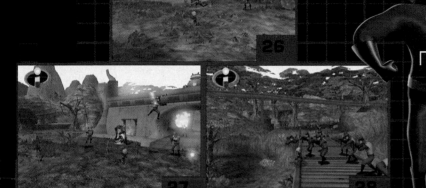

26

27

28

26. You must now destroy the four generators on the building itself—one at each corner of the building. Roll up the walls opposite the generators to gain momentum, then roll up the ramp under the generators to smash them.
27. After the second set of generators has been destroyed, the tower falls and the lasers blocking the door are removed. Roll into the building and up the broken tower.
28. Roll on to the bridge, straight through the henchmen gathered there.

TIP

When you reach the roof of the building, turn and roll around its outer edge. Destroy the third optional generator. This opens a gate back in the second clearing.

29

BONUS ITEM

Roll onto the track and head right toward the closed tunnel to grab the first bonus item at the very end of the track.

30

31

32

33

31. Turn right and roll up the ramp to the station. Stop at the top, near the traffic light.
32. Wait for the car to reach the station, then roll behind it on to the track.
33. Roll down the track, being very careful not to fall off the side. Don't turn too hard; use gentle taps to stay on track.

34. Enter the tunnel and take the side tunnel to the right to avoid being smashed by the approaching car.
35. The Incredi-Ball smashes a generator as it exits the tunnel. This opens the final gate in the main clearing.

BONUS ITEM

36. Before heading through the final gate, roll back through the very first gate you opened at the beginning of the level.
37. Turn right when you reach the next clearing. Head for the now open gate. Remember, you must destroy all three of the optional generators in the level for this gate to be accessible.
38. Roll through the cave. You will emerge near the second bonus item. Drop off the platform. You are back near the tower and can follow the same route out as you did previously.

39. In the clearing, roll up the ramp and through the gate.
40. Smash into any autoturrets and henchmen in your path as you roll toward the next station.
41. Stop near the light. Wait for the car to leave, then roll down the track.

42. The track is very twisting, so remember to turn gently so as to not fall off.

43. Roll into the tunnel. As you emerge, drop from the track to the ground below.

44. A horde of henchmen drops down from around the generator. Knock them into the generator to destroy it. This removes the lasers from the gate.

BONUS ITEM

Head toward the gate, but don't go through. Instead, turn right and roll down the small path. The final bonus item is at the end of the path. Return up the path to the previous area.

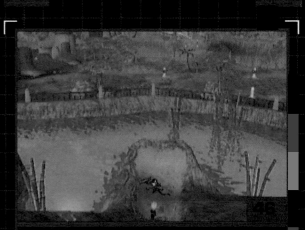

46. Go through the gate. The Incredi-Ball speeds down the hill toward the ramp below, and sails over the compound.

SECRET LAVA LABS
CHAPTER 18

MRS. INCREDIBLE

Enemies: NOMANISAN ISLAND HENCHMEN, LASER GUN HENCHMEN, FLYING LASER GUN HENCHMEN, FLYING MISSILE LAUNCHER HENCHMEN, LOBBER HENCHMEN

Mrs. Incredible seperates briefly from her husband when she finds herself in a labyrinth of underground lava tunnels, located underneath Syndrome's base. While her husband runs off in search of the rocket silo, Mrs. Incredible must find and activate the generator.

01. Run forward and up the steps. Use the console to open the door, then fight the henchmen in the corridor.
02. Proceed down the corridor to the lasers. Attack the two flying laser gun henchmen and then destroy the two generators next to the lasers. The lasers are disabled.
03. Move to the end of the ledge and use the hanging light to swing across the gap. Run to the console and activate the elevator.
04. Turn around and jump on to the elevator. Attack the flying laser gun henchmen that appear as the elevator descends.
05. When the elevator stops, jump across the gap. Use the console to open the door.

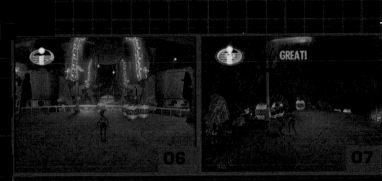

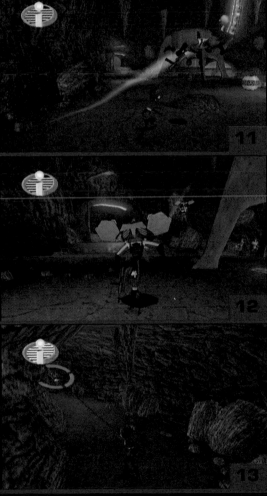

CAUTION

You can destroy the barrels in this area for health, but Mrs. Incredible isn't strong enough to destroy them on her own. Throw henchmen at them to break the barrels.

06. You enter the turbine room. You're about to face a fairly challenging and lengthy sequence of puzzles, all of which take place in this area.
07. Turn left in the turbine room and run between the barrels. A few henchmen guard this platform. Defeat them, and then move forward to the edge of the platform.

BONUS ITEM

Turn right at the entrance to the turbine room and jump over the railing. Attack the henchmen, and then grab the bonus item, which is hidden behind some barrels.

09. Two henchmen guard the island. Grab them and throw them into the lava.
10. Grab the handle hanging from the pipe and swing across the lava to the island.

11. Another henchman is stationed just ahead. Attack him and then move forward toward the door.
12. Two flying laser gun henchmen come through the door and two lobber henchmen stand under the turbine. Attack the flying henchmen first, then grab the bombs and throw them at the lobbers.
13. Use the console near the door and then enter the cavern. Run up the path, fighting the five laser gun henchmen guarding it.

17. Run up to the spotlights. Target the first spotlight and grab it. Mrs. Incredible pulls herself up on to the island. Release the light to drop down.
18. Quickly turn left and grab the second spotlight, then run forward and jump over the lava to attack the lobber henchmen.

CAUTION

You must cross the lava fairly quickly. The lobber henchmen are firing bombs and a single hit can knock Mrs. Incredible into the lava.

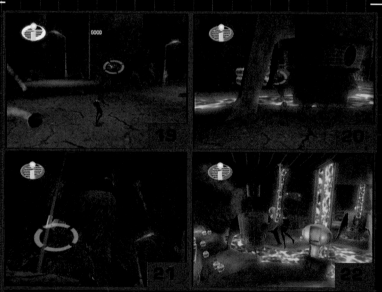

14. Use the console at the top of the path to open the door. Enter the control room. Two laser gun henchmen are stationed in the room. Fight them, grab the health power-up, and then use the console to activate the spotlights.
15. Two flying laser gun henchmen appear in the window that looks out on the turbine room. Attack them and then jump through the window into the room.

19. Attack the lobber henchman standing to the right of the third spotlight. Turn left and fight the two standing under the turbine. To the right, at the far end of this area, is a fourth lobber henchman.
20. After the four lobber henchmen are eliminated, run to the right end of the area and look across the lava near the turbine. If any henchmen remain standing on the opposite side, attack them.
21. Grab on to the third spotlight. When it reaches the top of its ascent, jump to the platform. Use the console to activate the mine carts.
22. Grab onto a mine cart and ride it over the lava. Drop down as the mine cart passes over the first turbine.

TIP

Before using the spotlights, turn right and attack any henchmen you see on the platform across the lava. The coming section is easier if you defeat everyone on the ground.

CAUTION

Do not ride the mine cart past the turbine! If
you do, it drops Mrs. Incredible down to the ground below.

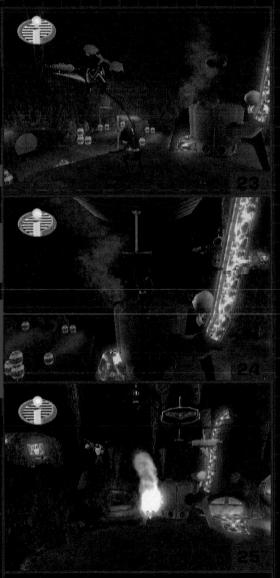

23. Punch the lever to start the turbine. Two flying
henchmen appear. Be careful . . . one of these
henchmen has a missile launcher, which not only
does a good deal of damage, it can also knock
Mrs. Incredible off the turbine. Attack the
henchmen as soon as they get within range.
24. Grab on to a mine cart as it passes. Now that
the first turbine is operational, it will carry Mrs.
Incredible to the second. Drop down on to the
second turbine as you pass over it.
25. Punch the lever to start the second turbine. Two
more flying henchmen appear, one with a laser
gun and one with a missile launcher. Jump over
any incoming missiles and fight them both as
soon as possible.

26. Ride a mine cart to the third turbine. Drop down and punch
the lever, then attack the henchmen who appear. This time,
it's a group of three flying henchmen. When they're defeated,
ride a mine cart to the final turbine.
27. Drop down and punch the lever to start the fourth turbine.
This opens a door below. Three flying henchmen appear. Fight
them and then drop off the turbine to the ground below.
28. Turn right and jump to the small island. Jump from the island
on to one of the rocks moving down the river of lava.
29. Stay on the right edge of the rock to avoid the two lasers in
the center of the cavern.
30. The rock follows the river around a bend. Immediately after
the bend, target the light ahead. Grab it before the rock falls
into the chasm.

PRIMA OFFICIAL GAME GUIDE

BONUS ITEM ◼

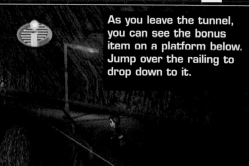

As you leave the tunnel, you can see the bonus item on a platform below. Jump over the railing to drop down to it.

Use the poles to swing back to the main path.

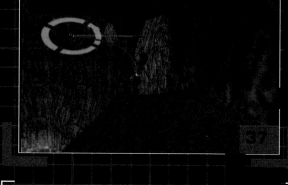

31. Swing forward and let go at the top of the swing. Grab the second light and then swing to the platform ahead.
32. Fight the henchmen (including the flying henchmen who appear behind you) and grab the health power-up. Then begin running up the path.
33. Proceed up the path to the three shielded henchmen. A group of flying henchmen appears to the left. Grab them and throw them at the shielded henchmen to clear the path. Finish off the flying henchmen and continue up.
34. A small group of laser gun henchmen guards a tunnel ahead. Fight them and move through the tunnel.
35. Lobber henchmen and laser gun henchmen guard the path beyond the tunnel. Eliminate them—you're very close to the top now.

38. As you approach the door, three flying henchmen attack. Quickly take them out, then use the console near the door and run through.

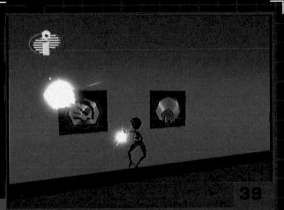

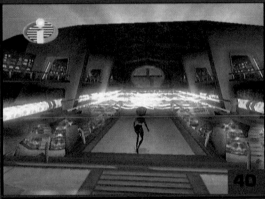

39. Proceed through the corridor, attacking the two wall turrets that appear on the right side. Continue forward and attack the pair of turrets that appear on the left. Use the console to open the door.

40. The room ahead is dangerous. Electrical currents sweep the walkway and lobber henchmen are stationed on the balconies on either side.

42. Before moving down the walkway, attack any lobber henchmen you can reach. Then run forward, jumping over the electricity into the gaps between the currents. Ignore the henchmen above. Run and jump forward as quickly as possible.

43. Attack the henchmen near the steps at the end, then turn left and run up the stairs to the balcony. Attack the remaining henchmen stationed here.

44. Run to the end of the balcony and use the console. This lowers the lights. Swing across the lights to the opposite balcony.

BONUS ITEM

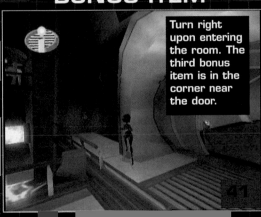

Turn right upon entering the room. The third bonus item is in the corner near the door.

TIP

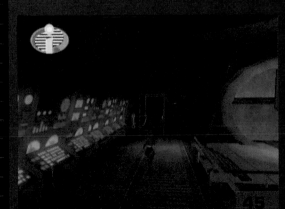

You can find health power-ups near the open doors at the end of each balcony.

TIP

If Mrs. Incredible is hurt, there's a health power-up in the corner at the top of the stairs.

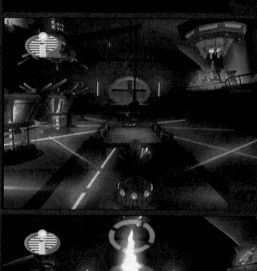

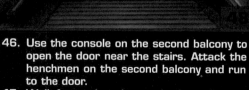

46. Use the console on the second balcony to open the door near the stairs. Attack the henchmen on the second balcony and run to the door.
47. Walk forward to the gap in the walkway. Target the ball above and wait for the electrical current to stop. Swing across quickly.
48. Walk to the next gap and target the ball. Once again, wait for the current to stop and then swing across. Run up the stairs to the right.

49. The next section can be tricky. You must walk on the small ledge, staying between the rotating currents.
50. Walk between two currents, then quickly move forward. There are three of these machines in all.
51. Use the console at the back of the walkway to lower the lights. Swing across the lights to the platform on the opposite side of the room.
52. To make it to the next console, you must jump through the machines when the current is off. Pay attention to the pattern of the electricity.
53. After the second burst of electricity in the first machine, run forward. Jump to the second machine. Wait for the third machine to fire its electricity, then jump to it when it's clear.

54. Jump to the platform and use the console to open the door.
55. Look up to the right of the console and grab the lamp. Swing to the platform and run out the door.
56. Use the console at the end of the short corridor to open the next door. Run through the next corridor, fighting the three henchmen stationed there. Use the next console to open the door.
57. Run up the steps and use the console to deactivate the electricity to the left. This console also starts the generator spinning and opens a door on the platform to the left.
58. Move to the left side of the platform and grab the generator arm as it moves toward you.
59. Swing from the arm to the next arm. Continue swinging from arm to arm until you can safely reach the platform.

TIP

Let go of one arm as soon as the next is automatically targeted. Double-tap the grab button to quickly let go and grab the next.

60. Go through the door and attack the henchman. When he's down, the next door opens. Go through and attack the two henchmen in the next room.

61. The next door opens, revealing a control room guarded by three henchmen. Attack them all, then grab the health power-up in the corner. Use the console to deactivate the second electrical field.
62. Return to the platform. The generator has started moving in the opposite direction. You must swing from arm to arm back to the entry platform.
63. Stand on the right edge of the platform and wait for a generator arm to come within reach. Grab it and swing from it. Swing from arm to arm to the next platform.
64. When you reach the platform, use the console to activate the generator. Step into the elevator to complete the mission.

ROCKET SILO
CHAPTER 19

MR. INCREDIBLE

Enemies: AUTOTURRETS, DOUBLE TURRET, ARMORED HENCHMEN, LASER GUN HENCHMEN, FLYING LASER GUN HENCHMEN, FLYING MISSILE LAUNCHER HENCHMEN, HELIBOTS, VELOCIBOTS, TANKS

While Mrs. Incredible runs off to start the generator, Mr. Incredible must make his way into the rocket silo and activate the rocket. This is an extremely combat-intensive level, so be ready for some serious fisticuffs!

01. Run up the steps to the door marked G6. Use the console to open the door and enter the corridor.
02. Run down the corridor toward the spotlights. When Mr. Incredible steps into the lights, he sets off a trap.
03. As soon as he steps into the light, lasers block off the hallway in both directions. Two pairs of turrets appear on the walls. Destroy the turrets to remove the lasers.
04. Continue down the hallway and use the console to open the door.
05. Enter the control room. Your first task is to fight all the henchmen, which won't be easy: A small army of armored laser gun henchmen occupies this room.

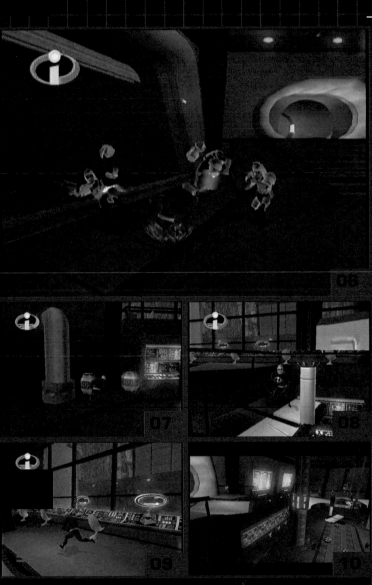

11. Activate the console nearest the entrance. Jump onto the lift, and ride it up.

BONUS ITEM

The first bonus item is right above the entrance. You can jump to it from the lift or use the cranes to reach it.

06. Use standard attacks to build up your Incredi-Power, then use a jumping Incredi-Punch to take out large groups.
If you need health during the battle, you can find a power-up behind the first column. Otherwise, grab it when the battle is over.
08. Run to the back left console and use it. This lowers the near-by lift. Jump onto the lift, then jump to the balcony.
09. Use both consoles on the balcony. The first causes the cranes above to drop their cargo. The second activates the door console on the opposite balcony.
10. Drop down to the floor and activate the console near the col-umn on the opposite side of the room. The lift partly lowers, but Mr. Incredible can't reach it yet.

13. Jump to a crane, then swing and jump to the next crane. Jump to the lift ahead.

17. Run down to the spotlights. It's another trap. Destroy the turrets, then run down the corridor toward the door.
18. A barrier drops from the ceiling, blocking the corridor. Lift the barrier and then use the console to open the door.

CAUTION

The remainder of this level consists of a series of increasingly difficult battles. Be ready!

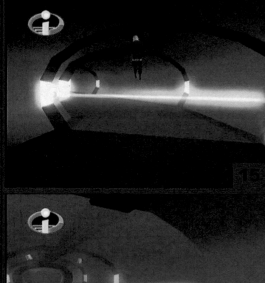

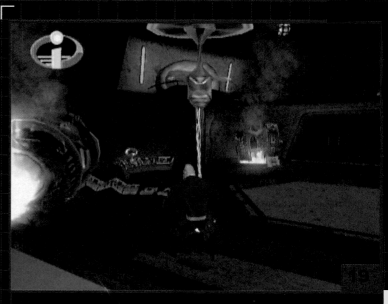

19. The first arena features a group of helibots that patrol in a circle. They appear in pairs and every time you destroy one, another appears.

14. The lift rises. Jump to the balcony and activate the console to open the door.
15. Enter the corridor. Jump over the first laser barrier.
16. Another laser barrier lowers from the ceiling. Roll under this second barrier.

TIP

If you use the active console, the cranes above drop their cargo, giving you more items to use as projectiles.

23. Eventually the helibots stop appearing. The center of the floor opens and a tank rises into the room.
24. This is a tough tank battle because of the close quarters. Get on the steps to avoid its lasers and the flamethrower; the extra height makes it easier to jump over the attack.
25. Be sure you move out of the way when you see its beam attack charging.
26. When the tank starts lobbing bombs, grab them and throw them back. Hit the tank with three bombs to destroy it.
27. The second console activates when the tank is defeated and the cranes drop their cargo. Use the console to lower the lift, then ride it up to the platform.
28. Jump and grab on to one of the moving cranes. Jump from crane to crane to the balcony on the opposite side of the room.

20. To destroy them, jump and punch them when they reach the lowest point in their pattern.
21. Alternately, use the debris scattered around the room as projectiles.
22. A health power-up is tucked away by the entry steps. Unless you absolutely need it, wait until after fighting the helibots to use it.

TIP

It's easier to jump from crane to crane if you jump just as the crane reaches the apex of its first swing (otherwise Mr. Incredible loses momentum). Pull in the direction you want to jump, just before letting go.

TAP ⦿ REPEATEDLY TO LIFT. PRESS Ⓐ TO DROP

29. Use the console and run through the door into the corridor.
30. A barrier drops, blocking the passage. Stand on the marker, lift it, and proceed.
31. Another spotlight trap is ahead, as well as three laser gun henchmen. This trap is slightly different. Two turrets appear on the right wall and two lower from the ceiling. Destroy them all to disable the barriers.

32. Attack the henchmen, then use the console to open the door.
33. You enter a large control room. Immediately head left and attack the henchmen near the console. Use the console.
34. Turn your attention to the flying henchmen. There are many of them, equipped with both laser guns and launchers. Use the crates to attack them or jump up and punch them when they get within range.
35. There's a console near the stairs, initially blocked by crates. Destroy the crates and use the console. This extends one of the bridges above.
36. Eventually, the console near the lift activates. Use it to lower the lift. Then ride up to the upper level.
37. Go up the steps and activate the console nearby. Turn around and run across the bridge. Grab the health power-up, then use the console to open the door.

NOTE

The next arena is optional. It gives you the second bonus item, but it is a fairly tough battle. If you want to skip it, wait for the second bridge to extend and then exit the control room through the other door.

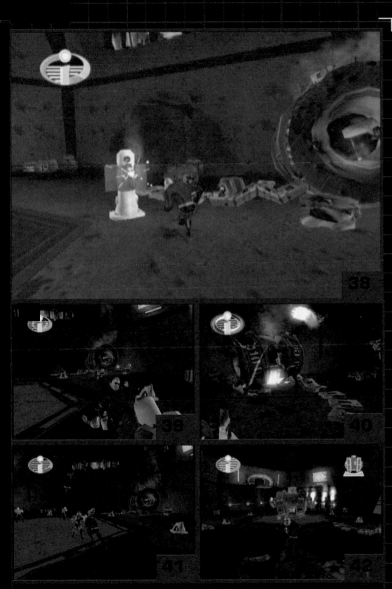

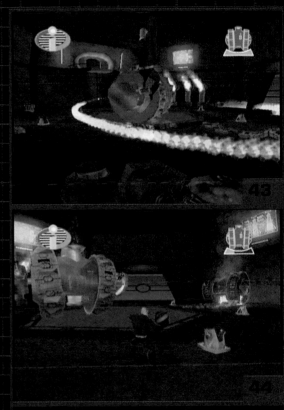

43. Use the standard tank strategy, dodging its attacks until it starts lobbing bombs. Hit it with three bombs to destroy it.
44. A second tank rises into the room. Repeat the process with the second tank.

BONUS ITEM

When the second tank is defeated, a door opens. Run inside to grab the bonus item.

38. Drop into the arena and immediately attack the autoturrets. Then turn your attention to the henchmen.
39. Attack all the henchmen on the ground. If you have the opportunity, grab them and throw them at the flying henchmen.
40. Attack the flying henchmen, using debris or jumping attacks when they fly low.
41. More henchmen appear in the center of the room. Keep attacking until all of the henchmen are defeated.
42. When the room is cleared of henchmen, a tank rises into the room.

TAP ⊙ REPEATEDLY TO LIFT. PRESS ⊘ TO

46. There is a console inside the newly opened room. Use it to lower the lift. Ride the lift back to the control room, and then run across the bridges to the next door.
47. Use the console to open the door and enter the corridor. Jump over the first laser barrier as it lowers, then do the same with the second.
48. A barrier drops from the ceiling. Stand on the marker and lift it.

49. A spotlight trap is just ahead. Destroy all four turrets to lower the barrier.
50. Run forward and fight the three armored henchmen, then use the console at the end of the corridor to open the door.
51. Grab the health power-up on the platform, then drop down to the floor. Immediately run around the center of the arena, attacking the autoturrets.
52. Destroy the double turret next, but don't pick it up just yet.

TIP

There's a health power-up just behind the double turret if you need it.

53. Before picking up the turret, try to destroy some of the velocibots flying around the room. This can be difficult. They move quickly and are hard to target with projectiles. Watch their shadows and use jumping punches or stand on the steps and use projectiles to destroy them. It's not easy, but taking out three or four before using the turret makes the upcoming section slightly easier.

54. After fighting the velocibots, stand on the marker and pick up the turret.

55. Immediately, a door at the back of the arena opens and several flying henchmen with launchers appear. Aim at their heads, firing just above them so they fly into your fire.

56. Concentrate your fire on the flying henchmen, then immediately turn to the velocibots.

57. The second door opens, releasing more flying henchmen and velocibots. Fire at them as they emerge. Henchmen begin flying from both doors, so keep a steady stream of fire aimed just above them to prevent them from reaching firing position.

58. A large group of armored henchmen appear on the center platform. Try and take them out quickly, then return your attention to the flying enemies.

59. A second group of armored henchmen appears in the center, along with several more velocibots. Keep a steady stream of fire on them, but don't let any flying henchmen reach firing position.

60. Shortly after the final group of ground troops arrives, you're prompted to drop the turret. Anyone remaining is around for the next fight, so if you can make one final sweep, do so.

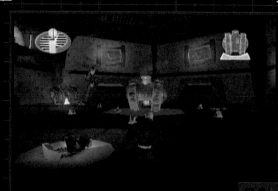

TAP ● REPEATEDLY TO LIFT. PRESS ⊘ TO DROP

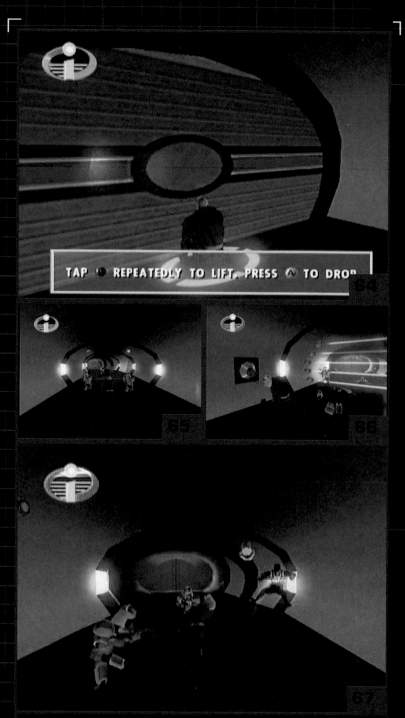

61. When you drop the turret, a tank appears in the center of the room. Throw the tank's bombs back at it to destroy it, but be careful—any remaining henchmen are attacking as well.
62. When you destroy the tank, the lasers blocking the exit are disabled.

BONUS ITEM

Find the third bonus item before leaving the arena. It is hidden in a tank hull along the edge of the room.

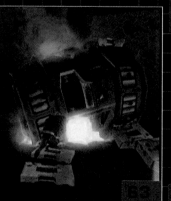

64. Use the console to open the door and run into the corridor. A barrier prevents passage through the corridor. Stand on the marker and lift it out of the way.
65. Run forward and fight the first group of henchmen.
66. Just past the first group is a spotlight trap. Destroy the turrets to disable the barriers.
67. Defeat the next group of henchmen. Another barrier lowers before the end of the hall. Lift it, then use the console to open the door.

PRESS ⊕ TO RELEASE DEVICE

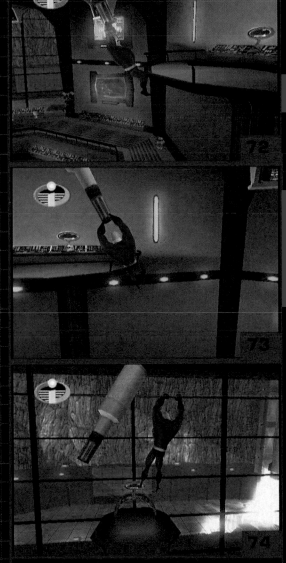

68. When you enter the large control room, immediately turn right and attack the henchmen on the walkway.
69. More henchmen emerge from a side room. Fight them all, then take out the flying henchmen by throwing projectiles at them.
70. Go down to the lower level and rotate all four devices. This starts the generator.
71. Stand on the ramp. When the crane arm passes by, jump and grab on to it.

72. Ride the crane up to the first platform. Jump from the crane to the platform and use the console.
73. Jump to the crane again and ride it all the way around the room to the platform on the opposite side. Jump to the platform and use the console.
74. Grab the crane and ride it to the platform near the large window. Jump to the platform and use the console. The rocket is now ready to be fired.

SAVE THE WORLD
CHAPTER 20

01.

02.

THE INCREDIBLE FAMILY

Enemies: OMNIDROID 10

This is it! The final battle. Mr. Incredible is not alone and has his family of superheroes at his side. Mr. Incredible's primary goal is to destroy the enormous, shiny, new Omnidroid sent over via rocket by Syndrome to destroy the city. Luckily, he has some help.

01. Fighting this Omnidroid requires a slightly different strategy than the one used on previous models.
02. The primary strategy you need to employ is dodging. The Omnidroid continually tosses vehicles and chunks of pavement at Mr. Incredible. As you run toward it, veer from side to side down the street to avoid being hit.

03. The Omnidroid also fires its two turrets. Dodge the lower one easily by running to the side or jumping over the shots. When you see the upper turret firing, immediately jump. An explosive blast follows its beam.

BONUS ITEM

As you run toward the Omnidroid during the first round, look behind the crashed trucks on the left side of the road for the first bonus item.

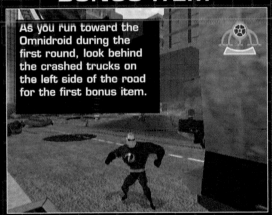

05. Run up the marker near the Omnidroid's foot and begin lifting. Violet and Dash speed to the rescue in the form of the Incredi-Ball!
06. The Omnidroid jumps to the opposite end of the street. Turn around and pursue it.

07. Run from side to side down the street to avoid the Omnidroid's constant barrage of boulders and vehicles.
08. Remember to jump away from its top turret beam. It explodes, doing damage to a small area.
09. When you reach the Omnidroid, grab some debris and toss it at the lower turret as it fires at the Incredi-Ball.
10. After the turret is hit, the Omnidroid stabs at Mr. Incredible with its legs. It stabs three times. The legs are slow; you can easily dodge them by running and jumping.

11. When the turret resumes firing, once again pick up some debris and throw it at the turret.
12. The Omnidroid again tries to stab Mr. Incredible three times. Repeat this exchange two more times, so that you've hit the turret four times total.

CAUTION

You must hit the turret four times before the Incredi-Ball runs out of health!

13. Violet and Dash race away and the Omnidroid jumps to the opposite end of the street. Turn around and pursue, once again running side to side and dodging its fire.

BONUS ITEM

As you pass the blue car and the RV on the left side of the street, run up the car and jump on to the roof of the RV to grab the second bonus item.

15. When you reach the Omnidroid, stand on the marker near its foot and lift.

TAP ● REPEATEDLY TO LIFT

16. This time, it's Frozone to the rescue. Turn around and begin running toward the Omnidroid, avoiding its turret fire and its projectiles.
17. As before, you need to throw projectiles at the turret when it is firing.
18. Also as before, the Omnidroid tries to prevent this by stabbing its sharp feet into the ground. This time, it stabs five times with each round of attacks.
19. Hit the turret four times to complete this round of the battle.

CAUTION

If Frozone runs out of health, the battle is over!

BONUS ITEM

20. During the Frozone-assisted section of the battle, look by the bus stop near the Omnidroid to find the third bonus item.

21. Mrs. Incredible is here to assist this time. Mr. Incredible has picked up the huge drill. Try to hold it steady and aim it at the Omnidroid.
22. When the drill is targeted on the Omnidroid, activate it. It sails into the Omnidroid, destroying it completely. Congratulations! You've officially saved the world.

BATTLE MODE

Battle Mode is unlocked once you've defeated the Omnidroid 09 in the "Great Falls" level. Battle Mode can only be unlocked for PlayStation2 and GameCube. Battle Mode needs to be downloaded via Xbox Live for the Xbox console. Battle Mode is a series of increasingly tough fights—nine rounds of intense brawling and bruising. You can play Battle Mode as Mr. Incredible or Mrs. Incredible.

Here are some tips to keep in mind while fighting through the troops: Never use regular Incredi-Punches if you can help it. Instead, use regular melee attacks, which increase your Incredi-Power. Then wait until you have enough Incredi-Power to use a more powerful Incredi-Punch on a large group of enemies.

After each round, you get a few health power-ups to ease your wounds. Just concentrate on standing up, round to round, and you should be able to make it through.

Here's are all the enemies you face in each round.

ROUND 1

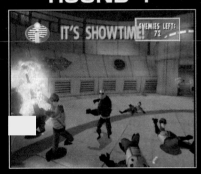

• **100 Nomanisan Island Henchmen**
The first round will get you warmed up. Remember to use standard attacks as much as possible in order to build up your Incredi-Power. Don't let the henchmen surround you (at least until you're ready to use your Incredi-Punches). There are 100 henchmen in all; after they're eliminated you move on to the second round.

ROUND 2

• **100 Armored Henchmen**
Things get more difficult in the second round. You have to defeat 100 henchmen, but these are armored henchmen and can take much more damage. Your basic strategy should be the same: use standard punches to build up your Incredi-Power, then let the henchmen surround you and let loose with an Incredi-Punch.

ROUND 3

• **5 Lobber Henchmen**
This is a brief respite from the tougher rounds. All you need to do in here is avoid the lobbers' bombs, then pick them up and toss them back at them. There are five lobber henchmen. When they're defeated, it's on to the fourth round and things get increasingly crazy.

ROUND 4

• **5 Lobber Henchmen**
• **Unlimited Nomanisan Island Henchmen**
You only need to defeat five lobber henchmen. Attack the henchmen as they come close, but try to get to the lobber henchmen before dealing with the rest. Otherwise, the melee henchmen will just keep coming. After the target number has been reached, clear the arena of any remaining henchmen to end the round.

ROUND 6

- **40 Laser Gun Henchmen**
- **Unlimited Armored Henchmen**

Imagine the previous round, but more difficult in every possible way. You must destroy the 40 laser gun henchmen which appear in small groups. Armored henchmen protect them and they don't count against your target tally. You must attack the melee troops or you'll be swarmed. Stay to the sides to get the laser gun henchmen as soon as they appear.

Build up your Incredi-Power with standard attacks and try to take out as many armored henchmen as you can while you wait for the next group of laser gun henchmen. When all 40 have been defeated, clear the arena of any remaining armored henchmen.

ROUND 8

- **1 Tank**

If you're playing through Battle Mode after finishing the missions, you should be fairly adept at fighting tanks. If not, remember to jump over the laser gun and flamethrower attacks, then move to the side as soon as the top turret begins charging. After the beam attack, the tank will begin lobbing bombs. Pick up one of these bombs and throw it at the tank. This will start its attack pattern from the beginning. Repeat this process three times to destroy it.

Remember not to get close to tanks. They have a powerful pulse attack that knocks you back and causes a good deal of damage.

ROUND 5

- **40 Laser Gun Henchmen**

The ranged attacks of the henchmen are the only real difficulty in this round. Keep moving around the arena, taking out the laser gun henchmen as they appear.

ROUND 7

- **3 Flying Missile Launcher Henchmen**
- **Unlimited Lobber Henchmen**

Though there are fewer enemies in this round, they are tougher to eliminate. You only need to defeat the three flying henchmen, but they're carrying launchers, making it a somewhat difficult task. Additionally, an unlimited number of lobber henchmen will fire bombs from the sides of the arena.

As Mr. Incredible, wait for the flying henchmen to fly past the entrance to the arena—this makes them much easier to target. Then throw a bomb as soon as they're targeted. As Mrs. Incredible, use stretch attacks to take them out quickly.

ROUND 9

- **1 Tank**
- **75 Armored Henchmen**
- **19 Armored Laser Gun Henchmen**
- **5 Lobber Henchmen**

Though this round is very difficult, it's not quite as difficult as it may seem. Why? Two words: friendly fire. Dodge the tank's attacks as normal, but save it for last. It will take out many of the henchmen that appear, especially with its bombs. Once the henchmen have been reduced to a manageable number, fight them or the tank normally. When the arena has been cleared, you will have conquered Battle Mode!

SECRETS

To enter these codes, pause the game and select "Secrets" from the menu. On the next screen, enter the code you wish to activate.

INVERTCAMERAY

Inverts the camera control on the Y-axis.

INVERTTURRET

Inverts aiming controls for turrets.

LABOMBE

Weakens the damage dealt by bombs.

LOSTGLASSES

Causes the game to become blurry. This code works only on the PlayStation 2.

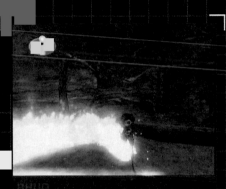

BHUD

Toggles the heads-up display on or off. No limitation.

BOAPLACE

Make the game 20 percent easier.

BWTHEMOVIE

The game goes into slow motion.

DANDRUFF

The henchmen launch their death shrapnel all the time, including when they are hit and anytime they nce.

DANIELTHEFLASH

Gives the player unlimited Incredi-Power, reduces enemy damage ability to half, and causes the player to d xtra damage to all enemies. The effects last for a limited time.

DEEVOLVE

Gives the active character a tiny head. This code does not work with the Incredi-Ball.

EINSTEINIUM

Gives characters giant heads. Not on Incredi-Ball.

EMODE

Turns on ethereal view. Works only on the PlayStation 2.

FLEXIBLE

Supercharges Mrs. Incredible with infinite Incredi-Power for a short time. This code has no effect on any other character.

GILGENBACH

Makes Dash invincible to damage from friction or collisions. Has no effect on other characters.

HI

Displays the Heavy Iron logo.

INVERTCAMERAX

Inverts the camera control on the X-axis.

PINKSLIP

Mr. Incredible lights plants on fire just by walking through them. Has no effect on other characters.

BASSMODE

The game is played in fast motion.

SPRINGBREAK

Henchmen bounce more.

TONYLOAF

Gives Violet infinite invisibility power for a limited amount of time. Does not affect other characters.

TOWNIE

Mr. Incredible glows when he swims. This code is available only on the PlayStation 2 and it has no effect on other characters.

UUDDLRLRBAS

Instantly gives the active character 30 health.

YOURNAMEINLIGHTS

Entering this code rolls the credits.

BONUS ITEMS

This section gives you the locations of all three bonus items in each level. Each bonus item unlocks one piece of artwork or additional FMV, which you can view by going to the gallery, from the main menu.

BANK HEIST

1. From the starting point, turn and run toward the elevated grate. The bonus item is on top of the grate.
2. Inside the bank, look on the desk in the back right corner.
3. Jump through the open window in the large, heavily guarded control room near the end of the level. The bonus item is on the ledge outside.

SKYLINE STRETCH

1. After the first ride on the police helicopter, jump through the gap in the fence on to the billboard's walkway. The bonus item is on the walkway.
2. Turn left immediately after entering the warehouse. The bonus item is hidden behind a shelf.
3. The third bonus item is in plain sight at the far end of the first U-shaped roof, just after the second police helicopter ride. Run straight after destroying the air conditioner.

BUDDY AND BOMB VOYAGE

1. As you approach Bomb Voyage's helicopter the first time, swing left and grab the bonus item hanging in the air.
2. Swing to the right as you pass the very last cable before the roof battle.
3. The final bonus item is located on one of the platforms of the roof during the boss battle.

APARTMENT INFERNO

1. Turn left at the very first pillar that you must lift. The bonus item is hidden behind a broken wall.
2. In the room with three pillars, jump up to the top of the fireplace after crossing the third pillar.
3. The third bonus item is in the hallway with the teeter-totter floor, near the ceiling.

LATE FOR SCHOOL

1. Jump to the right from the last gravel mound, just before the entrance to the tunnel.
2. After the tunnel, jump from the ramp over the semi trucks. The bonus item is on top of the truck in the center of the intersection.
3. After jumping the final intersection, veer right. The final bonus item is just behind the school bus.

BEACH LANDING

1. The first bonus item is behind the waterfall in the secret area before the first cable slide (see Chapter 9 for details).
2. Just before entering the lagoon at the end of the level, run across the fallen pole to the small outcropping.
3. The final bonus item is located on a small island on a lagoon.

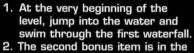

NOMANISAN ISLAND

1. At the very beginning of the level, jump into the water and swim through the first waterfall.
2. The second bonus item is in the secret cave near the first leaper-bot battle (see Chapter 10 for details).
3. Just before the level's exit, jump out on to the destroyed seeker-bot towers.

VOLCANIC ERUPTION

1-3. Items are in plain sight.

ROBOT ARENA

1. After the velocipod battle, drop down to the lower level of the arena. Turn left and break the wall.
2. After reaching the second check-point, turn left at the intersection and break the wall.
3. The third bonus item is in the back left corner of the tank arena.

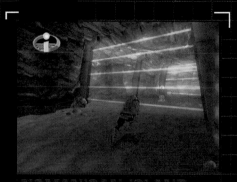

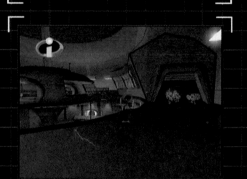

GREAT FALLS

1-3. Items are not in rocks and are not random.

SYNDROME'S BASE

1. The first bonus item is in the opening room. After the tank battle, you will find it in side room to the right of the exit, hidden behind some crates.
2. The second bonus item is in the corridor leading to electrical generator room in the last room on the left. You can access this room after using the second console.
3. Near the end of the level, after crossing the second bridge in the upper hub room, go into the room on the left. It is hidden behind crates.

FINDING MR. INCREDIBLE

1. After you activate the first console, the nearby elevator opens. The bonus item is inside.
2. In 1-D, you see the bonus item at the end of the hall. To get it, you must go to the control room in corridor 1-E and go through the door that opens inside. The bonus item is just outside this door.
3. The final bonus item is located behind the door on the fourth, optional platform in the upper level of the crane room.

100-MILE DASH

1. Take the right-hand path over the first tunnel, just before the first checkpoint.
2. The second bonus item is in plain sight on the path at the 42 percent mark, just before dropping down to the lower level.
3. In the caverns at the end, take the second path to the left just before the exit.

VIOLET'S CROSSING

1. The first bonus item is located on the outcropping. You see it after passing through the first gate, but cannot access it until passing by the second henchmen and running up the slope.
2. The second bonus item is located behind the building, right after the second checkpoint.
3. The final bonus item is located in a cave near the exit. Turn right at the final gate to find it.

INCREDI-BALL

1. Turn right on the first monorail track. The bonus item is at the end of the track near the lasers.
2. The second bonus item is behind the secret gate. You must find and destroy all three optional generators to open the gate. (See Chapter 17 for details.)
3. Just before moving through the final gate, turn right and go down the slope to find the bonus item.

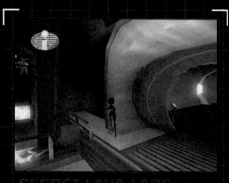

SECRET LAVA LABS

1. Enter the turbine room and turn right. Jump over the railing. The bonus item is hidden behind the nearby barrels.
2. As you move up the circular walkway after the lava river, look down after passing through the tunnel. The bonus item is just below the walkway.
3. Look right as soon as you enter the room with the lobber henchmen and the moving current.

ROCKET SILO

1. In the first control room, ride the first lift up to the ceiling and turn around. The bonus item is just above the entrance.
2. Defeat every enemy in the secret room at the end of the level. (See Chapter 19 for details.)
3. In the turret room at the end of the level, you can find the final bonus item inside one of the destroyed tanks.

SAVE THE WORLD

1. Look behind the crashed trucks near the center of the level.
2. Jump onto the RV to find the second bonus item.
3. Find the third bonus item behind a bus stop near the Omnidroid.

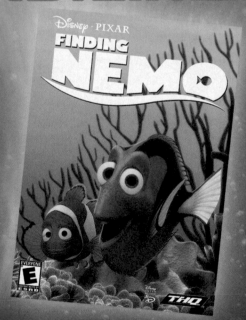

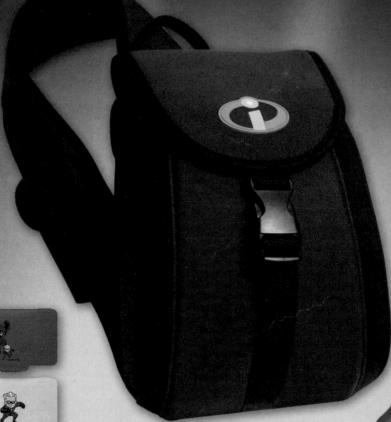